W. J. DAVIES

IMPRISONED BY OUR PRISONS

THE FABIAN SERIES

Series Editor Ben Pimlott

Forthcoming titles

Can Labour Win?
Martin Harrop and
Andrew Shaw

Competitive Socialism
Austin Mitchell

Goodbye Council Housing?
David Clapham

Messing up the Media
Peter Fiddick

Own Your Own
Oonagh McDonald

Reforming Whitehall
Clive Ponting

IMPRISONED BY OUR PRISONS

A programme of reform

Vivien Stern

UNWIN
PAPERBACKS

LONDON SYDNEY WELLINGTON

First published in paperback by Unwin Paperbacks, an imprint of Unwin Hyman Limited, in 1989.

Unwin Hyman Limited
15–17 Broadwick Street
London W1V 1FP

Allen & Unwin Australia Pty Ltd
8 Napier Street, North Sydney, NSW 2060, Australia

Allen & Unwin New Zealand Pty Ltd with the Port Nicholson Press
Compusales Building, 75 Ghuznee Street, Wellington, New Zealand

---

British Library Cataloguing in Publication Data

Stern, Vivien
Imprisoned by our prisons: a programme of reform. – (The Fabian Series)
1. Great Britain. Prisons
I. Title II. Series
365'.941
ISBN 0 09 175812 2

Typeset in 10 on 11 point Garamond by Saxon Printing Ltd, Derby
Printed and bound in Great Britain by Cox & Wyman Ltd, Reading

Contents

General Editor's Preface

Imprisoned by Our Prisons is published in the Fabian Research Unit's series of short books on past, and future, policy. The series has been launched in order to develop a genuine radicalism, based on principles of equality, fairness and collective responsibility. The studies are 'Fabian' in the sense of an interest in practicality: they will be concerned with the political and administative means of achieving goals. They will take no refuge in cautious moderation, but seek instead a rational extremism, exploring the limits of possible progress.

The series is connected to no party. Each study – by a distinguished political, academic or journalistic author – is a personal contribution. It does not necessarily express the views of the Fabian Research Unit or of the Fabian Society with which the Unit is associated.

Ben Pimlott
Director
Fabian Research Unit

Acknowledgements

Thanks are due to the many people who have helped in various ways to bring this book to fruition, especially Mervyn Barrett, Silvia Casale, Paul Cavadino, Iain Crow, Anna Donovan, David Faulkner, Stella Fry, Carol Gaca, Professor Norman Jepson, Jill Matthews, Rod Morgan, Eric Smellie, John Staples, Cynthia Stephens, Professor Hans Tulkens, Anne Webster, Melior Whitear and Jackie Stanley.

Particular thanks are due to Clare Gregory, without whom the book could not have been produced and to Tony Christopher. Three books have been indispensable in setting the scene: *The Fatal Shore* by Robert Hughes, *A Just Measure of Pain* by Michael Ignatieff and *Insiders* by Una Padel and Prue Stevenson.

Chapter 1
What is Prison for?

> Let us drink a good health to our schemers above
> Who at length have contriv'd from this land to remove
> Thieves, robbers and villains, they'll send 'em away
> To become a new people at Botany Bay.
>
> From the ballad "Botany Bay: A New Song" (1790)

Two centuries ago, at the end of the 1780s, a very important development in penal history took place. After a long and terrifying journey from Portsmouth, 11 ships carrying 736 convicted criminals dropped anchor at Botany Bay. This First Fleet led the way for 102,000 convicts altogether who made the involuntary journey to Australia. Many died, some even before the ships left Portsmouth – typhus was a constant risk – some during the journey. Neglect and ill-treatment during the period of servitude caused many more deaths. Some convicts were hanged for crimes committed during their convict years. The first to meet that fate was a seventeen-year-old boy called Thomas Barrett, hanged in Sydney for stealing "some butter, dried peas and salt pork".

Many more survived, to become farmers, traders, crafts people. They were of all ages and the range of their offences was wide. Petty theft commonly led to transportation. A labourer, Thomas Halliwell, ended up in Australia for stealing "one live hen to the value of two pence, and one dead hen to the value of two pence". Large numbers of the convicts came from Ireland. "Australia was the official Siberia for Irish dissidents at the turn of the century" writes one historian of transportation.

Age was no barrier to the imposition of such a harsh punishment. The oldest woman transported in the First Fleet was eighty-two. Nor was extreme youth. A nine-year-old chimney sweep who had stolen a pistol and some clothes was transported with the First Fleet.

Looking back over 200 years, the horrors stand out starkly – the journey, when the convicts spent days in irons, crammed into dark ill-ventilated holds; Norfolk Island, the final place of punishment for the real recalcitrants, where convicts were regularly beaten to death; Point Puer, the juvenile reformatory for children as young as nine.

Yet, for many, their prospects were more hopeful than they would have been in earlier years, when those convicted of a wide range of offences faced the prospect of the gallows. Hanging was available for over 200 offences altogether, including many against property. Stealing in a house or on a highway to a value above 40 shillings was a hanging offence.

Yet, by the late eighteenth century, the numbers going to the gallows were beginning to dwindle. In the years 1779 to 1788, 531 convicted offenders were actually hanged. But another 500 or so had capital sentences commuted or received the Royal Prerogative of Mercy. Hanging was becoming less acceptable so another way of dealing with convicted offenders was needed; and the problem of what to do with them was made worse by the American Declaration of Independence in 1775. Between 1717 and 1775 the American colonies received 40,000 British and Irish convicts. Then transportation in this direction ceased and convicts started to be crowded into decrepit naval ships, the hulks, moored on the Thames at Deptford and Woolwich and in naval ports such as Portsmouth. The politicians and civil servants were faced with the problem of what to do with them. The search began for an alternative destination. Various places in Africa were proposed and rejected. In 1786 the current head of the Home Office, Evan Nepean, put forward a plan to transport convicts to New South Wales, a place of which little was known. It had been visited only once before, sixteen years earlier, by Captain Cook.

Nevertheless the plan sounded on the face of it sensible enough. It would only cost 15 per cent more per head than keeping prisoners in the hulks and produce much less public alarm than the presence of these disease-ridden ships, prone to riot and escapes, close to towns and villages. It would put the problem of dealing with criminals out of sight and far away, where it would give little political trouble. It was accepted gratefully enough by the politicians of the day and on 13 May 1787 the First Fleet set sail from Portsmouth.

Transportation was chosen as the solution in 1787. But there was another option on offer – an option with many influential friends and supporters. Jeremy Bentham was one such enthusiast and in the very year that the convict Fleet set sail he began drawing up plans for a model prison or penitentiary, the Panopticon. The publication in 1777 of John Howard's *The State of the Prisons* had sown the seeds of a new view of prison – a prison designed not just as a holding place for debtors and vagrants, minor offenders and those awaiting trial, but as the central plank of a punishment system for criminals. The prison would at the same time strike terror into the hearts of prospective criminals and reform those subjected to its rigours. To reform them was essential because unlike hanging and transportation, both of which assumed the removal of the criminal for ever from the land, criminals sent to prison would eventually be released to live once again amongst the law-abiding. This argument was clearly put in the Penitentiary Act passed in 1779 which allowed the building of two penitentiaries:

> And whereas if many Offenders convicted of Crimes for which Transportation hath been usually inflicted, were ordered to solitary Imprisonment, accompanied by well regulated labour, and religious Instruction, it might be the means, under Providence, not only of deterring others from the Commission of the like Crimes but also of reforming the Individuals, and inuring them to Habits of Industry.

The two penitentiaries were never built and transportation to Australia filled the gap. But the supporters of the penitentiary idea remained true to their beliefs. As transportation became less popular, their moment came. In 1837, the government of the day set up a Committee, under William Molesworth, to enquire "into the System of Transportation, its Efficacy as a Punishment, its Influence on the Moral State of Society in the Penal Colonies and how far it is susceptible of improvement". The Molesworth Committee recommended that transportation should cease. It had failed on all counts. It did not remove the criminal class once and for all from British soil, because the terrible circumstances of the time pushed an endless supply of people into crime. It did not deter. In fact – and this was one of the main problems – for many of those sent there, their prospects were little worse, if not better, than their chances at home. Some indeed did make their fortunes in Australia in due course.

John Howard, Jeremy Bentham, the Quakers and the Radicals had won the argument. The Committee recommended that convicted criminals should be locked up in prisons. The new prisons were however not to be the overcrowded, filthy, disorderly dens of iniquity that John Howard had exposed in 1777, where once locked up, the prisoners had been left more or less to their own devices, guarded desultorily by corrupt gaolers ready to provide favours in return for payment, but otherwise at the mercy of other prisoners or gaol fever. They were to be more orderly and more specific in their assaults on the human being, not now primarily on the body, through chains and floggings, but on the soul, through solitary confinement and the silent system.

Experiments with solitary and silent systems had already been run, in Pennsylvania and New York. In 1842, England followed suit. Pentonville prison was completed, on a radial model soon to be seen in many more Victorian prisons, with each cell door being visible from a central point. Prisoners were to be kept separate. Each cell contained all that was needed for the inmate, table, chair, hammock, broom, bucket, mug and dish, soap and towel, a Bible and a cobbler's bench where eight and a half hours' work a day was done. Exercise and chapel alone required prisoners to leave their cells. But even then complex arrangements were made to prevent them seeing or coming into contact with each other. When leaving their cells for chapel or exercise prisoners wore brown masks with holes for their eyes. In chapel they sat in individual wooden compartments with high sides so they could only look forwards to where the Chaplain stood. They were to be preserved from contaminating each other and they were to strive to reform.

Imprisonment today

Thus began the movement in dealing with law-breakers that still rules today. The basic ideas of John Howard and Jeremy Bentham which gave us Pentonville, Wormwood Scrubs, Wandsworth and Strangeways in Manchester are also behind the building of, for example, Littlehey, a new prison in Cambridgeshire for 484 men.

And they continue to open: Full Sutton in Yorkshire for 447 men, the Mount in Hertfordshire for 484 men, Swaleside in Kent for 504 men, Garth in Lancashire for 512 men, Brinsford in Wolverhampton for 448 men under twenty-one. The list goes on. It is therefore none too soon to pose again a question which is often asked. The question is: where have we got to with prison as the centrepiece of society's response to law-breakers? Is the system working well? What have we learnt since Pentonville opened in 1842? What adaptations have we made? Should our dependence on prison continue?

Indeed there have been changes and adaptations over 140 years. Perhaps the most fundamental change is the complete loss of the original rationale. The idea of reforming prisoners through incarcerating them is quite dead. The system is still searching for an alternative rationale. So far it has found nothing more than a repackaged version of the 200-year-old aims of transportation. Prison removes the "evil" from our midst and inflicts punishment. Whatever vestigial notions of reform may have been left in the minds of the general public, no one involved in penal administration admits to the possibility that prison could, except in rare cases, be doing the recipients of it any good.

Most accept the basic contradiction inherent in imprisonment, that, in the words of a famous Prison Commissioner, Alexander Paterson, "it is impossible to train men for freedom in conditions of captivity". Most see only too clearly the results of taking people, usually from the least advantaged backgrounds, putting them in close confinement for some weeks or months with others from similar circumstances and then turning them out, stigmatised and dependent, into an unfriendly world. Penal administrators work to much more modest aims, to try and send prisoners out no worse than they came in, to reduce institutionalisation, to offer drug or alcohol treatment to those who want it, to equip people, if possible, with a marketable skill or educational qualification. Rarely are even these achieved. Some may at least find satisfaction in the thought that whilst prison does no good to those sent there, the community benefits from their absence from society for a while.

In spite of a constant flow of empirical evidence that prison does not reform, the demise of the rehabilitative rationale has been slow. The supporters of the Pentonville regime in the 1840s were disappointed at the recidivism rate and at the other side-effects of the system based on their ideas, the high level of insanity and suicide amongst the prisoners. Yet in 1895 belief that it could work was still undimmed. The Gladstone Committee which looked into the prison system argued that prison should be trying to send prisoners out of prison "better men and women, both physically and morally, than when they came in". More than sixty years later, the belief that good could come of it still flourished. A White Paper of 1959 quoted the Gladstone report and said, "The constructive function of our prisons is to prevent the largest number of those committed to their care from offending again."

Ten years later a new realism had crept in. The White Paper of 1969 described the overall aim of prison as the protection of society and described the obligation of prison services as doing "all that may be possible" to encourage prisoners to come out and lead a good and useful life. In March 1988 Home Secretary Douglas Hurd summed up current ambitions: "Our general aim is to hold an offender at the necessary level of security while preventing a deterioration in his attitudes and doing whatever is possible to prepare him to return to the community."

So, two centuries after the start of transportation, the problem of dealing with criminals, which perplexed politicians and writers in the 1780s and the 1830s, is no nearer solution. Current remedies are regarded as no more successful than transportation was in 1838. The corner stone of the whole penal system is a massive and costly enterprise, the prison system, informed overall by no higher ambition than to send people out in no worse position than when they came in. And in most cases, it does not even achieve that.

Is prison effective?

What can be said about the effectiveness of prison? What part does it play in the control and prevention of crime? How are we going to justify the continuation of the eighteenth-century idea into the twenty-first century? At the simplest level, is it having any beneficial effect by stopping those who go to it from committing crimes again? The answer is straightforward. It is not. Fifty per cent of adult men, nearly 40 per cent of women, two thirds of young male offenders, eight out of ten juvenile offenders leaving custody are caught and reconvicted of another offence within two years. Over a quarter of the adult men and four out of ten of the young men are back inside a penal establishment by the time two years is up. Not a high success rate by any standards.

Perhaps, though, the failure rate of those actually subjected to the experience is not the point. For, it is sometimes argued, the justification for sending people to prison, although it is accepted that it does them no good, is the deterrent effect it has on the rest of us. It is worth having one out of every 1,000 of us incarcerated if it keeps the other 999 out of trouble.

Unfortunately, there is no evidence at all that would justify such a conclusion. Research suggests that tough penalties can deter, but usually only at the bottom of the scale of offences. Such measures as car clamping are effective, but even then, with all the cost and inconvenience of being clamped, every day many car owners take the risk. The streets of London have not been cleared of illegal parkers. Different people and groups are likely to react very differently to penal measures designed to deter. Deterrence assumes some rational calculation. Many crimes are committed in circumstances where the strength of emotions or influence of drugs such as alcohol overcomes any rational approach to the deed. When sentencing for a particular offence has changed to become harsher there is no evidence that crime rates have been affected at all.

Deterrence also assumes some knowledge of the likely outcome of committing particular offences, the likelihood of being sent to prison, the likelihood even of being caught. Research suggests that the state of such knowledge is very low. The British Crime Survey, a major Home Office research study, found that only one in five had any idea what proportion of adult male burglars went to prison. Most respondents underestimated the severity of the courts.

Neither can the argument that prison is the only thing standing between most people and crime be sustained. For many it is internal controls that stop them committing crime. Also most people have much more to fear from committing crime than temporary loss of liberty. Conviction for a crime, even without a prison sentence, can mean loss of reputation, and job, and rejection by family and friends. Conversely, some have nothing much to lose, and something to gain. One of the women interviewed by Una Padel and Prue Stevenson for their book on women in prison described a childhood of being in care from the age of three, followed by foster parents, an approved school, remand centre, borstal at eighteen, prison and prison again. At age twenty-seven, after several sentences, she said:

> Prison just made me worse ...; I wasn't frightened of it. Sometimes, in a sort of way, I was glad to be in, when I couldn't cope on the outside. I was used to it. I didn't have to make any decisions. It's when you get out that the problems really start.

No doubt the fact of prison has a deterrent effect. No doubt the use of prison for certain crimes expresses the moral outrage people feel towards certain criminal acts and reinforces morality. But this effect cannot relate directly to a particular level of imprisonment. It cannot depend on whether today 94 out of every 100,000 people in England and Wales are locked up, 37 out of every 100,000 as in Holland, or 264, as in the State of Texas.

So we are left with containment. Does prison protect the public by keeping out of circulation dangerous and violent people? Here the answer is clearer. Imprisonment can achieve such protection. Very serious offenders are locked away, and escape very rarely, though even with such cases there are difficult questions to resolve. How long do such people remain dangerous? How is dangerousness to be judged? How is deterioration to be prevented as the years of a very long prison sentence pass by?

Such people, however, constitute a very small proportion of those in prison. Out of a prison population of around 50,000, 390 adult male prisoners, 3 women and 10 young offenders are deemed to be Category A, that is those "whose escape would be highly dangerous to the public, the police or the security of the State". Even the next category, Category B, those "for whom the very highest conditions of security are not necessary but for whom escape must be made very difficult", constitute around 4,800 adult men. And the widely held view is that categorisation is over-cautious.

A fifth of those sent to prison every year have committed offences involving violence. Four fifths have not. Nearly half of those in prison on any one day are there for burglary, theft, handling stolen goods, fraud or forgery. Nearly half are serving sentences of eighteen months or less. Three quarters of the men over twenty-one sent to prison are sentenced to eighteen months or less. In 1980 the Home Office published a research study into the incapacitation effects of imprisonment. It concluded that reducing the use of prison would have a negligible effect on the crime rate. The Home Office itself, in its handbook for sentencers, says, with characteristic caution but nevertheless some firmness, "No realistic increase in prison terms would make a substantial impact on crime rates by virtue of locking up the particular offenders caught, convicted and sentenced".

The conclusion is inescapable. The overall amount of imprisonment has no measurable effect on crime rates. It cannot have any effect. There is a relationship at the most serious level: Over 90 per cent of homicides are solved and long prison sentences follow conviction; 75 per cent of serious violent and sexual offences are solved. The application of the penal system to the rest of criminal activity is haphazard and selective. Crimes reported to the police represent, if the figure from the Home Office British Crime Survey is accepted, perhaps a quarter of all crimes perpetrated. For these, a police clear-up rate of 33 per cent means only one in three is solved, by finding and charging an offender. The Home Office has calculated that perhaps 5 per cent of all crimes end up being dealt with by a court. For the less serious offences, the outcome once in court is a bit of a lottery. Chances of a prison sentence can vary from 8 per cent in Rotherham to 23 per cent in South Tameside, 9 per cent in Newcastle to 28 per cent in Sunderland.

The offence of burglary is a good example. In 1984, 28 per cent of recorded burglaries were cleared up. Of those burglars coming before the court, 31 per cent got an immediate prison sentence. In the magistrates courts burglars' chances of going to prison can vary (according to a Home Office research study) from 7 per cent in one magistrates' court to 47 per cent in another.

A direct relationship between the use of prison and the control of crime is therefore, except at the level of the most serious offences, difficult to establish, though it is often argued, quite reasonably, that a high use of prison increases crime through turning petty criminals into more serious ones.

Too much prison

We are faced therefore with a strange phenomenon. We have a very expensive commodity, with an average cost per recipient of £252 per week, and a capital cost per each new prison cell of between £46,000 and £69,000, which does very little good in any terms. After achieving the very limited objective of protecting the public by taking out of circulation about 400 very serious offenders and about 5,000 (at a generous estimate) people who could present a serious risk, it has very little else to offer to crime control, to public protection, to deterrence, to the maintenance of law and order.

This point of view is widely held. The Chief Inspector of Prisons said, in a report published in April 1988:

> "Ultimately the choice may lie between less or shorter use of custody and further heavy demands on the exchequer for additional accommodation. How much longer the taxpayer will continue to favour the latter solution is open to question, but if a cost benefit analysis is any guide, the balance should tip decisively in favour of less use of custody and far shorter terms for most of those coming before the courts."

A Conservative Party study group report on prison said:

> First, it is doubtful whether the extensive use of incarceration has any real influence on the actual or future incidence of crime. Indeed, the relationship between the penal system as a whole and the level of crime is tenuous and uncertain; and no causal connection can be established with confidence.

Douglas Hogg, the Home Office Minister responsible for prisons, told a group of magistrates:

> We will always need prisons. But we do, as a nation, need to get away from the habit of regarding prison as the only "real punishment"... Particularly for a teenager who has not embarked on a life of crime there is really very little sense in imposing a gaol sentence which can result in him spending his time sharing a cell with two more experienced crooks, to emerge after 6 months or a year as a more proficient criminal than when he went in.

Roy Hattersley told the House of Commons on 30 March 1988:

> "The problem is the number of people sent to prison in this country ... we send too many people to prison and keep them there for far too long."

Yet, in one of the most surprising decisions to be made by a Government committed to cutting public expenditure and getting value for money, the amount of prison available is to be not stabilised at its present level, not wound down, but vastly expanded. Plans have been laid for a growth in the number of prison places by 22,000, an increase over 1983 of 55 per cent, at a capital cost of one billion pounds, conservatively estimated. These additional places will be in new prisons – twenty-two new prisons are planned between 1988 and 1995 – and in new-built extensions to existing prisons. Yet, in spite of this vast expenditure, those wanting to see an end to the use of cells built in the 1840s or even earlier, an end to prisoners being denied access to lavatories, an end to the use of buildings where "occasionally waste pipes allowed raw sewage to overflow on to landings" (Durham prison), where "prisoners and officers frequently have to paddle through other men's urine towards the end of the 'slopping out' session as the drains cannot cope with the volume of use" (Wandsworth prison), will be disappointed. The prison building programme is not a replacement programme. The billion pounds is not being spent to transform the conditions in Wandsworth prison, or in Durham. These old insanitary buildings are not to be closed as a result. In fact by the end of the century, 14,500 prison places (a quarter of the total) will still not have integral sanitation.

This is the major plank of prisons policy – expansion, making room for more and more prisoners. The Home Secretary confidently told the House of Commons:

> The doubling of expenditure on prison building that we have accomplished since 1978–79 is clearly necessary after the years of neglect, and all the projections show that those places – and, indeed, more places – will be needed. We need not regret that spending decision in the least. It is not for the Home Secretary, Government or the House to lay down to the courts how many people they send to prison. It is our job to provide places for them.

Private sector prisons

Along with this massive investment in locking up property offenders goes an entirely new development, the involvement of the private sector in incarceration. In 1987 the Adam Smith Institute published a report, *The Prison Cell*, on the US experience of private sector prisons which ended on an optimistic note. "Private prison experience in America", they said, "has been sufficiently extensive and positive to warrant a major experiment with prison privatisation in Britain. Britain has led the world in most areas of privatisation, yet in the prison field there is a danger that she will fall behind as countries such as America and France use privatization to solve the major social problems of public-sector prison decline". They went on to suggest that "bids from the private sector should be invited for the construction and operation of new prisons", with a new centre for London being the top priority. They also called for two secure juvenile establishments and three medium security adult prisons to be contracted out. They suggested that prison industries should be replaced by a variety of private sector enterprises, some run by prisoners. US firms should be invoked to advise on British privatisation. Existing prison staff wanting to become private providers should be given preferential treatment, and if it is all sucessful, full privatisation of the whole prison system should be gradually introduced. Also in 1987, in May, following a visit to the United States, the House of Commons Home Affairs Committee published a report, supported only by the Conservative members, advocating that as an experiment the Home Office should enable private sector companies to tender for the construction and management of prisons, in particular of new remand centres. The Chairman of the Committee was Sir Edward Gardner QC who left the Commons at the 1987 General Election.

In March 1988 it was announced that a new private company, Contract Prisons Plc, had been set up by Rosehaugh Plc (a property development group), Racal-Chubb (the security company which supplies the prison service with locks) and Pricor (an American company which designs and contract-manages prisons in the USA). The new company claimed it could build a prison and have it ready for use within three years. The Chairman of the company is Sir Edward Gardner QC

The Government's response to these recommendations was tentative. Replying to the Home Affairs Committee's report, the Home Secretary indicated how far he was currently prepared to go. A new Prison Building Board had been set up with private sector representatives on it. The Board had invited forty or so interested companies to submit proposals to build new urban remand centres and open prisons.

Private sector involvement in building prisons is not controversial. Private sector management is. When the proposition that the private sector should run prisons was first floated by the Adam Smith Institute in 1984, it was greeted with some amusement and incredulity. Now it has become a real possibility, there is a temptation to welcome it. After all, could prisons be worse? It might constitute the shock the system needs to force it to change. Certainly, in the short term at least, it would probably improve conditions and prisoners would probably welcome it. It would require standards to be drawn up and adhered to. If private prisons had a code of standards to follow, public prisons would surely have to follow suit. Why then is it so to be resisted?

First, it is to be resisted because of the dangers of the creation of a powerful, wealthy lobby interested in increasing the size of the prison population. Imprisonment cannot be allowed to become subject to market forces, a commodity which brings more profits as it grows. Second, prisoners cannot be handed over by the state to private organisations who would be given control over disciplining them, punishing them, recommending them for parole or deciding on the shape and content of their prison sentence.

A doubly dangerous path is therefore being followed – a vast expansion of prison places and an invitation to commercial bodies to start taking an interest in the penal system. The objective is to get more places, quickly. Expanding the system is the top priority. Policy developments on improving the prisons, tackling the enormous gulf between the performance of the system and the aspirations set out for example in the international instruments to which the UK has subscribed, receive scant attention and are accorded little importance. The process of planning, building, staffing and opening new prisons sweeps all before it. What happens inside these places of incarceration is of much less moment. The prison administrator responsible for opening a new prison on time will be very well regarded. The prison administrator who manages to win a right for a few more prisoners to make phone calls to their families cannot expect such warm approval. The decision to expand the prison system by 55 per cent is not only misguided in terms of crime control. It also perpetuates unthinkingly, and sets solid in bricks and mortar, all the elements that make the British prison system one of the most repressive in Western Europe.

Chapter 2
What is Wrong with the Prison System?

> The purposes of the treatment of persons in custody shall be such as to sustain their health and self-respect and so far as the length of sentence permits, to develop their sense of responsibility and encourage those attitudes and skills that will assist them to return to society with the best chance of leading law-abiding and self-supporting lives after their release.
>
> *(The European Prison Rules, Basic Principle Three)*

Prison systems are never easy to run. They possess a number of features which taken together add up to a managerial and administrative nightmare. Possibilities abound for the abuse of the weak or powerless by the strong or powerful. Justifications such as the need for security and staff safety, the imperatives of management, and the requirements of administration are always at hand to excuse denials of prisoners' basic human rights. Resort to secrecy by the management is endemic. The temptation is always there to hide the truth about what is going on behind the high walls and locked doors, a temptation aided and abetted by the Official Secrets Act. Yet secrecy of another sort is needed – the secrecy that protects prisoners from the ever-prying eyes of the journalists eager to find a story – a story for example on how a noted celebrity took to prison life or what privileges a particularly notorious prisoner is getting.

Each of the components of a prison system brings with it a cluster of inherent difficulties. First of all, there are the focus and centre of the whole system – the prisoners. A small minority finds going to prison a respite, a haven, a place of comfort and warmth compared with the park benches and cardboard boxes of a hostile outside world. For most, even the highly experienced, it is a time of stress, anxiety and fear. Suicide prevention has to be a major preoccupation of the prison authorities. Many prisoners are very unexceptional people, maybe the unlucky ones who got caught, just wanting the prison experience to pass quickly and quietly. But others are weak, inadequate, vulnerable, their offences arising from severely damaged personalities. Some are overbearing and prone to violence, tending to prey on those least able to look after themselves. A few are convicted of such well-publicised or heinous crimes that they need protection from other prisoners twenty-four hours a day.

Then there are the staff, doing a thankless and often highly unpleasant job, with strong feelings of being undervalued by their employers and looked down upon by social acquaintances. They try to meet conflicting expectations simultaneously. On the one hand they are supposed to run prisons firmly and clamp down on any signs of disorder. On the other they are expected to help prisoners and prepare them for life on the outside. Frequently they are understandably frightened by what prisoners might do if they had the chance. There are strong pressures to be loyal and conform to the group, as well as all the temptations faced by anyone who is given considerable power over people who have been degraded and humiliated.

Next there is the plant, a motley collection of unsuitable buildings. There are buildings built as castles and dungeons in earlier centuries. Parts of Oxford prison date from 1071. Dartmoor prison was originally built in 1815 by prisoners taken in the Napoleonic wars. There are examples of all the fashions in prison architecture, ninteenth-century galleried prisons, twentieth-century hotel corridor type prisons, converted country houses and old military camps with rows of Nissen huts.

Some prisons start off as one thing and end as another. Albany, a top-security prison on the Isle of Wight, started off being built in 1975 as a medium-security prison to replace Dartmoor. Stocken prison was originally designed as an establishment for young people under twenty-one, based on the ideas of the 1960s. It was put on ice until 1979 and then taken off the shelf. Building began in 1982 without rethinking or modification. Eight months before it opened it was decided that it should not be a youth custody centre after all but should cater for adult men.

Then there has to be taken into account the potential for controversy and scandal that surrounds all prison matters. Everything that happens in a prison system is of political interest. A notorious prisoner gets parole. Is it right that such a person should get parole? A rock group goes in to a youth custody centre (a youth prison for fifteen- to twenty-one-year olds) to give a performance. Is it fair? What about law-abiding youngsters? Do they get free performances? In Holloway women's prison there is a swimming pool. Why should these women have access to a swimming pool when they are supposed to be being punished? Such debates are regularly fuelled by one of the sure ways in which ex-prisoners can make a few pounds on release – by selling some revelations to a newspaper about sex and drugs in prison.

Overcrowding

The problems of the prison system in Britain are formidable. Furthermore, any strategy to confront them is diverted and confounded by overcrowding. Overcrowding has beset the system since the Second World War and provides a permanent barrier to improvement. The administrators of the system are continually pulled back from any attempts to do new and exciting work with staff and prisoners to managing the crisis. Their energies have to be used to find places to put down beds. They have to defer the closure of a decaying wing for refurbishment for just another few months. They must continue to use buildings more fit to be condemned. They try negotiating with the Ministry of Defence for unwanted army camps. As a last resort, they prevail upon a reluctant police service to keep prisoners in cells in police stations, for which the police receive payment of £1,008 per prisoner per week.

Overcrowding has been getting steadily worse. In 1966 the system was 6 per cent overcrowded. In 1977 it was 11 per cent overcrowded and in 1987 the figure was 15 per cent. The surplus population is not, however, spread evenly amongst all prisons. It is concentrated in the big prisons in the major cities, the prisons that serve the courts, called "local prisons" by the prison service, where short-term and remand prisoners are housed. Its effects are therefore much more severe than if it were spread over the whole system. Leeds prison, for instance, regularly holds more than twice the number of prisoners that it has room for. On the other hand Albany, which as a top-security prison houses some very long-term prisoners, has a stable population of around 300, fewer than the 311 there is technically room to accommodate.

Perhaps the full implications of being locked in a small cell measuring around 12 feet by 7 feet, with two other human beings for most of the hours in every 24, are brought out most starkly in a recent report by a prison Board of Visitors, the watchdog body of lay people appointed by the Home Secretary to each prison. Writing about Wandsworth prison, the Board comments on the sanitary arrangements:

> Defecation in the cell bucket, quite apart from degradation for the individual, obviously creates appalling conditions afterwards. Prisoners take avoidance action. Waste products are wrapped in paper and thrown out of the window... In order to solve the "parcels" problem the fixing of

wire meshes over cell windows has commenced. This, of course, makes things worse for the prisoners.

Overcrowding puts pressure on already inadequate facilities to the point where the minimum one bath or shower a week cannot be provided, supplies of prison clothes run out, exercise is reduced to a minimum. At Leicester prison, the Board of Visitors noted in its annual report the impact of overcrowding – cuts in staff training, the closure of the pre-release course for prisoners, reductions in education, attempts to give some prisoners exercise in an exercise yard no bigger than an alley or in "low-ceilinged rooms nobody would choose for a gym".

The prison population

Who are the people locked up in this overcrowded, creaking system, put away in places physically cut off from society, separated by high walls with bulges on top to foil climbers, and with entry by outsiders governed by detailed rules and regulations? Symbolically prison represents rejection by society. Nevertheless it reflects society, magnifying and highlighting its unresolved ambiguities, its cruelty or viciousness, its selfishness and neglect, its prejudices, inequalities and injustices. So it is no surprise to find the prison service receiving from the courts not a cross-section of society, but a population skewed towards the urban male poor, the young, the underprivileged, the abused, vulnerable, sick and addicted, the mentally disturbed and those discriminated against in the wider society.

Black people are particularly over represented in the prison population. The figures are alarming. When they were first made available they showed that in 1985 the proportion of black people in prison was disproportionate in all respects – among men and women, among young offenders and adults. The proportions were twice as high as the proportions in the general population for men and even higher for women. There were differences in sentence lengths and in the number of previous convictions between white and black prisoners which could not all be explained by differences in seriousness of offence. Black defendants were also less likely to get bail. The total of ethnic minority prisoners in 1985 was just over 12.5 per cent for men and 17 per cent for women. In 1986 these figures had risen to 13.5 per cent for men and 18 per cent for women. In 1987 the proportions had again risen to 14 per cent for men and 23 per cent for women.

The processes that lead to this outcome are clear. Disproportionate numbers of black people live in the poorest areas and suffer the worst housing, highest rates of unemployment and poorest educational opportunities. Their chances of being caught up in the criminal justice system are therefore much higher. And within the criminal justice process – through decisions to stop and search, arrest, prosecute or caution, decisions about the appropriate charge, whether to give or withhold bail, what happens at the court appearance, the sentence given and then eventually the granting of parole – there is the possibility of racism influencing the outcome. The cumulative effect of a series of racist decisions is the grossly disproportionate black prison population.

Within prison too, the potential for racist decision-making is substantial. The successful *Alexander* case showed this all too clearly. John Alexander was a black prisoner who complained of racial discrimination at Parkhurst prison because he was refused a job in the prison kitchen. The court case showed that while black prisoners formed 22 per cent of the prisoners in B wing, the only wing from which applications for kitchen work could be drawn, none was working there: "In my opinion", said Judge Whiteley at Southampton County Court, "the reason was that white prisoners at that time would not accept black prisoners working in the kitchen ... and the prison staff up to November 1983 were not prepared to remedy the situation by approving the appointment of black prisoners in the kitchen." The reports prepared on John Alexander were also cited in evidence. His initial assessment from Wandsworth prison where he had started his sentence said: "He displays the usual traits associated with people of his ethnic background, being arrogant, suspicious of staff, anti-authority, devious and possessing a very large chip on his shoulder which he will find very difficult to remove if he carries on the way he is doing."

His report at Parkhurst echoed these sentiments exactly. The judge found that these reports "contained racially discriminatory comments" which had the effect of "not treating Mr Alexander as an individual but as a damaging racial stereotype". The judge found for John Alexander and awarded him a sum in damages which was increased subsequently by the Court of Appeal.

The incident of which John Alexander complained took place in 1983. Time will tell whether the efforts made by the Prison service since then, through issuing an official prison service statement against racism, establishing a training programme and instituting ethnic monitoring of all decisions affecting allocation of prisoners to work and education can produce an environment where racism does not operate to get black prisoners the worst deal. Progress though does seem to be slow. The independent Chief Inspector of Prisons, who inspects about twelve prisons a year, found a gloomy picture when he inspected Stocken, a brand-new prison only opened in 1985, where presumably everyone was at least starting off trying to do everything right. Neither of the officers responsible for race matters had been on a training course. There was only one black member of staff. There was no race relations committee or support group. An extensive local staff training programme had no race relations content and "there was evidence that some staff used racially derogatory language".

Women in prison

Most prisoners are men, 96 out of every 100. Women prisoners are therefore a small minority and there are only twelve women's prisons for the whole of England and Wales. Scotland and Northern Ireland each have only one. The ambiguity with which society views the imprisonment of women is perhaps symbolised by the story of Holloway prison. The redevelopment of the old Holloway was announced by the Home Secretary in 1968. On the basis that, as he said, "most women and girls in custody require some form of medical, psychiatric or remedial treatment", the new Holloway was to be primarily a secure hospital. By the time it was finally built – the last bricks were laid in 1985, fifteen years after the original design was first agreed – other ideas prevailed. Buildings designed for treatment converted badly to buildings designed for punishment and there have been problems ever since.

The number of women prisoners is small. Yet, most of the women sent to prison are serving sentences for non-violent offences. Forty per cent of the female prison population are there for theft, handling stolen goods, fraud and forgery. The corresponding figure for men is half that. Burglary accounts for another 20 per cent of male prisoners whereas it accounts for only 5 per cent of the women prisoners. Women also seem to be sent to prison early in their criminal careers. Thirteen per cent of those sent to prison in 1986 had no previous convictions compared with 5 per cent of men. Nearly half the adult women who went to prison in 1986 went there for not paying a fine.

So, not only is the female prison population disproportionately composed of minor property offenders, first offenders and fine defaulters; the women in it also suffer from its position as a small adjunct to a large system run mainly by men and catering mainly for men. Since women's prisons are so few and widely scattered over the country, women are likely to be placed many miles from their homes. Women from London can be placed in Durham or Styal in Cheshire. Women from Newcastle can end up in Bullwood Hall in Essex.

Women pose even more difficult problems for the prison service because they have babies. In the year 1986–7, sixty-two women prisoners gave birth to babies in outside hospitals and returned to prison afterwards. Many women prisoners are the mothers of pre-school aged children. A census taken in August 1986 showed that 340 women prisoners between them were mothers of 455 under-fives.

What to do about women who are about to have or who have just had babies presents an impossible dilemma for the prison service. Should new-born babies be separated from their mothers? Clearly not. Is a prison the right place to bring up a new-born baby? Clearly not. The prison service tries to solve the dilemma by taking both decisions. Some mothers can keep their babies for a while. There are three mother and baby units. At Holloway and Styal babies can stay until they are nine months old. At an open prison in Yorkshire, Askham Grange, babies can stay until they are eighteen months old, But not all mothers will be allowed these facilities. Only those who will be due for release before their baby reaches nine months (if they are at Holloway or Styal) or eighteen months (if they are at Askham Grange) are eligible. And then the decision will be influenced by other factors as well. Are there other children already in care? Is there "a reasonable prospect" of the mother caring for the baby outside? If not, according to Home Office Circular Instruction 51/83, "it will be in the best interests of the baby for separation to take place within the first four weeks if the baby is not being breast fed, or at the end of the first four weeks if he is".

The inevitable conclusion is that mothers with new-born babies should not be in prison at all. They should be paroled, released, or dealt with some other way. But such a conclusion is regarded as unacceptable. Why, it is argued, should pregnancy and motherhood lead to leniency? Surely, it is said, women would become pregnant just to escape a prison sentence. So no solution is found and the status quo remains. Some mothers keep their babies with them and bring them up for their first nine to eighteen months in prison. Others have them taken away shortly after birth. Such a circle is frequently travelled in debates on prison matters, a circle that goes from an intolerable situation round to an unacceptable solution, then on to living with a status quo that no one finds acceptable.

Remand prisoners

The way remand prisoners are treated is also intolerable – and widely agreed to be so. Yet it has gone on for many years. Remand prisoners are those not yet tried or not yet sentenced. Those not yet tried are still, technically, innocent. Their guilt of any offence has still to be proved, yet their treatment is in many ways worse than the treatment of convicted prisoners. The proportion of remand prisoners rises steadily, 14 per cent in 1980, to 23 per cent in 1987. There are two reasons for the increases. First, more people are remanded in custody before their trial. Second, it is taking longer for cases to come to court. In 1980 the waiting time was 36 days for men and 25 for women. In 1987 it was 57 days for men and 44 days for women. And these averages conceal some very long remands. In 1987 one remand case took more than fifteen months to come to court.

Remand prisoners are held in the worst conditions the prison system has to offer in the overcrowded local prisons. Different rules govern the incarceration of remand prisoners. These allow, for example, more visits than are allowed to sentenced prisoners – one visit of fifteen minutes per day. They are, however, steadily being eroded. The rule allowing remand prisoners to have food brought in for them by visitors was withdrawn in March 1988. For "operational reasons" a visit every day is no longer available to many remand prisoners. At Leeds prison, for instance, where nearly 700 remand prisoners are held, daily visits ceased in 1986, as they did also at Ashford. And after such an experience of imprisonment, four out of ten of the remanded men and six out of ten of the remanded women do not receive a prison sentence at all. A small number are acquitted. The rest receive some other sentence or disposal of the court.

Mentally disordered prisoners

The holding of mentally disordered people in prison is another example of how the system goes round this circle and comes back to living with a status quo that no one finds acceptable. Outrage at the holding of mentally disordered people in prison is a feature of all official reports on the prison system. The Expenditure Committee in 1978, the May Committee in 1979, the Home Affairs Committee in 1981, the Prior Committee in 1985 all complained about the holding of mentally disturbed people in such an unsuitable place as a prison. In 1985 and 1986 the Social Services Select Committee of the House of Commons looked in more detail at what could be done. They obtained a figure of 1,500 mentally disordered male prisoners, though they doubted its accuracy. The proportion of women prisoners similarly suffering is estimated to be even higher. At Bedford prison they were told that "a severely disturbed prisoner had recently spent almost eight months naked in a stripped cell". When the Committee itself visited Bedford, they saw "a prisoner lying in a catatonic stupor with only a sheet for covering in an empty cell smeared with filth".

The Hull Board of Visitors in its report for 1987 describes the life of prisoners in Hull with serious behavioural or mental problems who "have to live a solitary existence lost in their own fantasies and depressions". Outrage is also regularly expressed by the judiciary when they find they are given no alternative but to send someone into a totally unsuitable environment. In a recent case the Common Sergeant of London protested vigorously that a man with a mental age of seven found guilty of sex offences had spent eight months in prison because no place could be found for him in a psychiatric hospital. Some mentally ill remand prisoners do not even get to the understaffed hospital of the overcrowded local prison. In another case lawyers protested that a client of theirs, suffering from paranoid schizophrenia, was sharing a police cell in Grimsby with two others and was not receiving his medication.

Yet it goes on. We have all – judges, official commentators, prison-system managers – managed somehow to live with this abuse, scandal, disgrace, affront for many years.

Mental disorder is not the only health problem prisons have to deal with. Drugs is another. The number of drug misusers in prison is high. The reasons why this is so are obvious. Drug misuse is itself against the law. Furthermore, the need to finance a drug habit can drive people to commit theft, fraud, burglary or robbery. The number of drug-dependent people sent to prison every year is estimated to be around 4,000.

AIDS in prison

The prevention and control of HIV infection and AIDS in prison is a new problem which throws into sharp relief some key questions about health, health care and prison management. Up to March 1988 the prison system had identified altogether 164 HIV positive prisoners. One prisoner died of AIDS in 1985. Home Office policy is set out in a memorandum of July 1987. When they arrive at the prison all new prisoners are questioned by a member of the hospital staff to see if they are in a high-risk category. If they are they will be sent to see the prison doctor. The doctor will discuss the possibilities and the prisoner can then have a test if he or she agrees or requests it. Those prisoners identified or suspected of being HIV positive are to be allowed "to participate in the normal regime of the prison as fully as is consistent with ensuring the health and safety of staff and fellow inmates". This means they should be in a single cell or sharing only with other prisoners identified as HIV positive. Specific cells may be "designated" for this purpose (ideally cells with integral santitation). All operational staff should know which are the "designated" cells – but prisoners should not be told. Such prisoners may also be subject to some restrictions on normal activities such as not working with machines or knives, not working in the prison kitchen and not engaging in physical contact sports. Prisoners subject to these restrictions have VIR (Viral Infectivity Restrictions) stamped on their files. Prisoners who develop symptoms will normally go to an outside hospital specialising in treating AIDS cases.

The memorandum has an interesting paragraph on confidentiality. It makes it clear that "government policy is strict on the need to preserve medical confidentiality in relation to AIDS/HIV antibody positive cases". However, this policy is a bit difficult when it comes to prisons. It goes on, "the particular circumstances of prisons place on the Department a responsibility to ensure, on grounds of health and safety, that staff with an operational 'need to know' are informed of the presence and identity of inmates who have been placed by the medical officer in Viral Infectivity Restrictions". This, of course, the memorandum argues, does not really give the information away since VIR is also stamped on the files of prisoners carrying Hepatitis B. Furthermore, "the Department also considers that it has an obligation to make such information available on a similar basis to police officers and others within the criminal justice system who have an operational 'need to know".'

The need to control and prevent AIDS, and care for and manage within the prison system people infected with HIV antibodies or suffering from AIDS, highlights many of the contradictions and tensions inherent in managing Britain's prisons. We see an initial wish to pay regard to human rights, a recognition that it would be desirable for prisoners not to be singled out, that tests cannot be compulsory, that hygiene is of the greatest importance, that confidentiality should be maintained and that the measures used for education and prevention in the wider community should be applied to prisons. Then the realities of the system close in. Prisoners must be singled out and treated differently because otherwise the prejudices of staff and prisoners will take over and their fate will be worse. Blood tests are not compulsory but those in a high-risk group who exercise their right and refuse a test may be subject to the same restrictions as if they had been tested and found positive. Hygiene is of the greatest importance for people who need desperately to avoid infection. Yet people infected or already showing symptoms are required to live in some of the most unhygienic buildings and conditions that exist for human habitation. Confidentiality would be desirable but the prison doctors, people who in other circumstances would regard it as axiomatic that information about their patients was confidential, are employed by the Home Office and are part of the management of the prison service. They therefore have to balance the interests of the patient with another interest, that of the smooth and proper management of the institution where they work. And the management requires them to breach confidentiality. The education available in the wider community stresses "safer sex" and advocates the use of condoms. Condoms are not available in Britsh prisons. In fact they are regarded as "contraband". It is a punishable offence to possess a "contraband" item. Furthermore, since conjugal visits do not take place in British prisons and condoms would therefore only be needed for homosexual activity, by issuing them, it is argued, the Government would be condoning an offence. Homosexual activity is only not an offence if it happens in a private place. No part of a prison is, it is deemed, private. Therefore all homosexual activity in prison is unlawful and the issue of condoms would be encouraging unlawful acts. The Home Secretary's view is that the idea of making condoms available "fails to take account of all the relevant factors, including the effect which a resulting increase in homosexual activities would have in terms of risk to HIV infection and otherwise". Incarceration dramatises and makes much more complex the handling of a problem already fraught with difficulty.

Long-term prisoners

For the prison system there is also the special difficulty of handling those who have been sentenced to very long terms of imprisonment, terms so long that even when parole is borne in mind, no end can really be envisaged, no plans outside prison can be worth thinking about. Expectations have to be narrowed to the prospect of a move to another prison, a downgrading of security category, pursuing a course of education perhaps, otherwise nothing but existing for perhaps the next 7,300 days. Or there is the choice of taking another path, deciding to fight back, not to give in to the system, not to obey the rules, to keep mind and spirit alive through resistance.

Long-term prisoners pose problems to any prison system. They have little to lose by not conforming. They have a great fear of deteriorating, of becoming passive and vegetable-like. The keeping up of relationships on the outside gets steadily more difficult. The British system has not found this problem easy to deal with. After the prisoner disturbances of 1972 a plan was developed to set up "control units" for disruptive prisoners. The units were intended to be harsh and punitive, or in official language "intentionally austere". The plan for the units assumed an initial stage of ninety days of almost complete segregation. If completed satisfactorily, the second ninety days would be slightly more benign. Misbehaviour would mean going back to the start of the ninety-day programme. The proposal brought forth a storm of protest and was quietly abandoned soon after it started. Sensitivities about the control units are still acute. When a group of experienced prison governors and administrators produced a new set of proposals for dealing with long-term prisoners and advocated that they should be dealt with in small units, they were at great pains to point out that nothing like the old control units of the 1970s was envisaged. The small units they advocated are being set up and outside academics are involved in their evaluation. Their relative success so far is encouraging but precarious, as the prison service faces dealing with people for whom sentences are getting longer and for whom the prospects of parole are being whittled away. In 1983 Leon Brittan announced at the Conservative Party Conference a new policy on parole. Normally, prisoners were eligible for parole after serving one third of the sentence. Following the announcement those sentenced to more than five years' imprisonment for an offence involving violence or drug trafficking would only get parole in "wholly exceptional" circumstances. Furthermore those convicted of murder in the course of robbery, who had murdered police or prison officers or committed sexual or sadistic murders of children would normally serve at least twenty years. A challenge to the courts on the propriety of the new parole rules was lost. The Home Office estimates that by 1987 these restrictions and a tougher policy on parole overall had already increased the prison population by 2,000.

Children in prison

Finally, at the opposite end of the spectrum from long-term prisoners convicted of serious offences, the prison service is required to cater for children, some as young as fourteen years old. Few regard the prison system as the right place for fourteen-, fifteen- and sixteen-year-olds, certainly not those who provide the service, the prison governors, who have consistently argued that such young people would be more appropriately dealt with elsewhere. Yet there are still nearly 4,000 young people a year aged fourteen, fifteen and sixteen being subjected to the most severe penalty available to the courts, mostly for non-violent offences. They are locked up, mixing with young offenders up to the age of twenty-one and vulnerable to all the bullying, sexual abuse and criminal education that is inevitable in such an environment. Some are in adult prisons, awaiting allocation to a suitable place.

Managerial failure

So prison administrators start off with a range of disadvantages not of their own making when facing their task of running a decent and humane system in even minimum conformity with international obligations – overcrowding, having to receive all the people no other agency wants, the victims of neglect and lack of facilities elsewhere, the victims of discrimination elsewhere, bad people, sad people, ill people, children, women in an advanced stage of pregnancy, the guilty and the innocent.

Some would say that the problems are so formidable that the failure over the past ten years to run a system that delivers a minimum level of service is understandable and excusable. Others would not. The managerial failure is certainly remarkable and in spite of current attempts to grip it, likely to persist for many years. On every performance indicator – number of prisoners working per week, number of prisoners attending education classes, hours spent by prisoners out of their cells, number of community involvement activities undertaken by the prison service – the system has deteriorated over the last ten years.

A look at the Chief Inspector's Report on Brockhill remand centre is an illuminating illustration of the way the system works. Brockhill was opened in 1965, a purpose-built centre to cater for young men aged up to twenty-one on remand. It was built with the worthy aim of taking young people on remand out of the overcrowded decaying local prisons. When the Chief Inspector's team inspected in June 1987 it was overcrowded, holding 263 in places for 163. Everyone was sharing a cell. There was no integral sanitation. Some places were in dormitories. The dormitories were a cause of concern because they gave great scope for bullying and intimidation. Plans to convert to cells in 1985 had been postponed to 1990. The windows and mattresses were vandalised. The small upper dormitory produced "a sense of shock: the floor was pitted and cracked, the walls were dirty and in one corner the flooring was particularly bad with a stench of urine coming from a number of pots, one of which was full". Two fifteen-year-old boys spent most of the day in this dormitory with nothing to do, waiting to be sent somewhere else.

Workshops had been provided but long ago converted to other purposes. Many prisoners wanted to work but no work was available. A little PE was available. There was education for about fifty prisoners but the statutory minimum of exercise time was not always given. Nor was there much recreation. Eating meals was done in cells. "Thus", concludes the Chief Inspector, "the majority of inmates spent most of the time locked up and idle." Clean clothes were not always available even once a week. The towels were dirty and damaged because prisoners used them to stop up holes in the broken windows. In the hospital was a hallucinating schizophrenic patient who had been there for three months. A prisoner coming up before the governor for a hearing on a disciplinary charge "sat on a low cardboard chair in front of the desk in the adjudications room." Two officers stood over him looking down at him ... "We were told", says the Chief Inspector, "that arrangements would be made for an inmate to make notes if he asked but we were not persuaded that, under the circumstances, anybody would dare to ask." The Chief Inspector concludes "no one appeared ready to challenge the depressing assumption that things could only get worse".

Obviously, following up such a report, heads are banged together and action is taken. Conditions at Brockhill were improved. Repairs were done. Cleaning was carried out. Clean clothes were issued twice a week. More education became available. More time was spent in recreation. Longer visits from friends and families were allowed. However, a prison establishment can only expect a visit from the Inspectorate every ten years, so such conditions could go on for a long time before being remedied

Similarly depressing is the report on prison industries by the National Audit Office. The report, published in 1987, was mainly concerned with the losses sustained by prison industries, though admitting that the provision of work for prisoners has other objectives than commercial ones. Some useful facts nevertheless emerged from their review. In 1977 nearly 16,000 prisoners were working in prison workshops. In 1986 the figure had fallen to just over 9,000. In 1976 17.6 million hours were worked. In 1986 the figure was 8.5 million. At one prison new workshops costing £1 million were finished in 1984 but had not been used for work by the time of the Audit Office's visit in 1986. At a brand-new prison opened early in 1985 only 115 work places were available for 295 prisoners.

Perhaps one of the underlying reasons for the difficulties faced by the service is the lack of any rationale that can be communicated to those working in it. The Chief Inspector, commenting on the causes of the disturbances in 1986 where prisoners rioted and put 800 prison places out of action, felt the need "for a start to be made on rekindling a sense of unity and common purpose within the prison system". It would be hard for staff to be excited or inspired by the official list of the functions of the prison service published in the 1983 Annual Report. First, this states the resources given to the service by Parliament must be used efficiently. Second, prisoners must be kept inside when they are meant to be inside and be got to court when so required. Third, prisoners must be provided with the basic necessities of life and something to keep them occupied. Finally, they should be able to keep their links with the community and be prepared to return to it "where possible".

Contact with the outside world

The lack of amenities, the low morale of staff, the struggle to maintain basic cleanliness and decency all matter to prisoners. But for the vast majority what perhaps matters most is maintaining contact with the outside world, keeping in touch with family and friends, not being forgotten by those outside, still being important to people beyond the closed world and not of that world. And here the inhumanity and oppressive nature of the British system is particularly striking. Take for example the rules on correspondence. It cannot, one would think, be harmful to write a lot of letters. It could even be helpful. Someone with humanitarian instincts might feel it could ease the pain and unhappiness caused by deprivation of liberty. Someone more utilitarian could regard it as a useful part of maintaining the links so necessary for post-prison resettlement. Someone with no higher aspirations than to run a peaceful, relaxed, trouble-free prison might regard prolific letter-writing favourably. Yet letter-writing for many prisoners is severely rationed, and incoming and outgoing letters are read.

Letter-writing is not, of course, the only way of keeping in touch. In society telephones are also now widely used. They are to be found in 82 per cent of all households. In fact telephoning has almost ousted personal letters as the normal mode of communication. Yet the simple matter of allowing prisoners to make phone calls is not simple at all – it is a matter of enormous difficulty. In many countries it is taken for granted. In Holland, for instance, all prisoners have access to telephones: in open prisons there are telephone boxes scattered around the complex of prison buildings and in closed prisons the call is made by a prison officer and then transferred to aprisoner waiting in a telephone booth. In Britain it has been a slow process. In 1984, pay phones were installed in Scottish prisons for low security prisoners. In 1986, for the first time, prisoners in open prisons in

England and Wales were allowed to use the phone. In 1988, this was extended to Category C, some women's and young offenders' establishments. Special telephones were installed, which allowed prison officers to listen in to calls.

The telephone conversations may allow at least a little privacy in maintaining relationships. Visits to prisons by family and friends cannot do this. They take place in large visiting rooms, usually across a table, within the sight though not the hearing of a prison officer. Sentenced prisoners over twenty-one are entitled to a 30-minute visit every 28 days, i.e. six and a half hours a year. The under twenty-ones are entitled to twice that: two 30-minute visits every month. Most prisons allow longer but about 8 per cent of adult convicted prisoners only get the minimum six and a half hours a year.

Visiting a prisoner is not easy. Prisoners can be located many miles from their homes. Prisoners who move out of the local prisons into a training prison will probably end up in a remote rural location, ill-served by public transport. Visiting a prisoner in a local prison in a city can mean a cold, wet wait standing conspicuously in the street outside the main gate, before visiting time begins.

This deprivation of all privacy in carrying on one's most important relationships – letters read, visits in a large public room under the eyes of prison officers – is an important element in the worst feature of the prison system, the way it strips the individuals subject to it of their dignity, individuality and rights. Prisoners become bodies, to be counted in relation to the capacity there is for them, given a number, pushed into ill-fitting clothes, and never away from the eyes of others. Even those lucky enough to be put in a single cell are all subject to the spyhole in the cell-door. And they are totally at the mercy of others for everything they need. Standing Order No. 4, published for the first time in 1985, is headed, very significantly, "Privileges". A privilege, so the document says, "may be defined as a facility or activity approved by the Secretary of State and permitted at the discretion of the governor, whose decision will be based on the availability of resources and the management requirements of his establishment". These "privileges" may also be forfeited, as punishment for committing an offence against the disciplinary code.

Prisoners' rights

The privileges are various. For example, prisoners may spend a certain amount of their private cash in any twelve-month period. There is a list of things it may be spent on: for example, games, watches, cards, calendars, batteries and toiletries. Prisoners may receive one daily, one Sunday, one weekly newspaper and two periodicals. Religious, educational and technical periodicals do not count towards this allowance. All these must come direct from the publisher, newsagents or booksellers. The governor can stop them if the contents "could present a threat to good order and discipline". Prisoners may apply for a general notebook and a drawing book and such applications "should normally be granted". A prisoner may ask for another but if the first one has not been filled, the request "may be refused". The notebook and drawing book will be "withdrawn" if they are misused or contain material "likely to jeopardize national security". A prisoner may take a notebook or drawing book out on release unless it has anything in it about prison staff, prisoners or crime.

No corresponding Standing Order called "Rights" exists, though prisoners do seem to have one right, the right to send a petition to the Home Secretary with a complaint about their treatment. Trying to complain about something that happens in prison is not easy. Not only do the authorities have in the end discretion about almost everything, complaining to any independent body about the way this discretion is used is fraught with pitfalls. The normal avenue is through the internal machinery. First the complaint goes to the appropriate prison officer. Then it can go to the governor. Or it can go to the watchdog body, the Board of Visitors. But Boards have very limited powers to do anything about an internal decision. The next stage would be to petition the Home Secretary. For the Home Secretary, of course, read an official in the Home Office who deals with petitions to the Home Secretary. This can take a long time. New monitoring procedures have been introduced to speed it up. The speeded-up procedures trigger a reminder to the Home Office if nothing has happened after two months and another reminder if no reply has been forthcoming after five months.

That is the internal route, with Home Office officials at the centre responding for the Home Secretary to complaints made by prisoners about decisions made by other Home Office officials. At no point in this chain does a non-Home Office employee or appointee feature. A prisoner can also choose the external channel and complain to an MP. The MP might be energetic and care about prisoners. So the complaint might be pursued vigorously. Otherwise it will be passed to the Home Office who will pass it to the department which deals with the petitions to produce a reply. The Home Secretary will sign it and send it to the MP who will then pass it on to the prisoner.

The only way to break out of this Home Office-controlled circle is to take the complaint to a lawyer. If the complaint involves or implies improper behaviour by a prison officer, this is also the only way to avoid being caught in the "false and malicious allegation" trap. It is an offence against Prison Rules to make a false and malicious allegation against a prison officer. When a prisoner makes such a complaint a warning is therefore given. If it can be proved to be true, there is no problem; if it cannot or is likely not to be, the prisoner can end up in trouble. Having weighed up the chances of being able to prove the truth of the complaint and the risk of facing a disciplinary charge, many prisoners may decide it is probably wiser to keep quiet and do nothing. And indeed this is what they do. All studies of the way the complaints system operates have concluded that the existence of the rule is a deterrent to legitimate complaints. It gives prison officers greater protection than other similar workers. It is not found necessary in other countries. It has always been argued by prison reformers that it should be abolished. The latest recruit to the cause is the Chief Inspector of Prisons who recommended its abolition in the report on complaints procedures.

The absence of any independent check or accountability is particularly marked in the powers the system gives itself to deal with those deemed to be troublemakers. First there is Prison Rule 43. Rule 43 allows the governor, "where it appears desirable, for the maintenance of good order or discipline or in his own interests, that a prisoner should not associate with other prisoners" to put such a prisoner in segregation. Once in segregation the conditions are almost as spartan as those being undergone by prisoners segregated for punishment after going through the disciplinary procedures. Yet the prisoners segregated by the governor for the sake of "good order and discipline" have gone through no procedure, had no reason given, are not entitled to know the reason, nor to know how long it will last or what they could do to be allowed back in the normal prison. The Board of Visitors has to authorise such decisions. Some are very conscientious about it. Others less so.

Those deemed to be most serious troublemakers in the eyes of the prison authorities can be subject to more draconian treatment. They can become "10/74s". These are the prisoners that the system deals with under regulations set out in Circular 10/74. The regulations allow the governor of a top-security prison "in an explosive situation to remove a subversive prisoner at short notice and without obtaining permission from officials". The prisoner is sent to a secure, usually a local prison, for a twenty-eight-day cooling-off period. Special cells are kept for the purpose in prisons like Wandsworth. The prisoners are then kept in segregation under Rule 43. The end result of this system is that difficult prisoners that no one wants are shunted round the system. They go for example to Wandsworth for twenty-eight days. Then they are due to go back. The sending prison declines to have them back. They either stay at Wandsworth for much longer than is appropriate, or are sent off for another twenty-eight-day sojourn somewhere else.

The limitations of these mechanisms are clear enough and have been highlighted many times. A report by the lawyers' organisation Justice, published in 1983, found grave defects in the current system and argued for far-reaching reforms in the statutory framework, complaints procedures and disciplinary procedures. The Chief Inspector's review of complaints procedures concluded that current procedures were not "fair, effective or widely known".

The total and continued resistance by the Home Office to any independent element operating in the prison system is a persistent theme running through the failure of most attempts at prison reform. Their resistance to the creation of an independent Prison Inspectorate is a good example. The idea of an Inspectorate was first mooted in 1978 by the Expenditure Committee of the House of Commons. It was repeated by the May Committee in 1979 in spite of strong Home Office opposition. The Home Office opposed not only an Inspectorate independent of the Home Office but even one within the Home Office but separate from the Prison Department.

The May Committee rejected these arguments and recommended an Inspectorate, separate from the Prison Department. Such an Inspectorate was set up in 1981. In his final report Sir James Hennessy, who retired as Chief Inspector in 1987, surveyed the first six years and commented on some difficulties. Before Inspectors' reports can be published they have to be considered by the Prison Department. This process was sometimes taking up to a year. By the time reports were published they were out of date and their edge was blunted.

Most recently the idea of an independent prison ombudsman has provoked a similar reaction. The Home Office argues strongly against it. The main arguments used by the Home Office are familiar. How would such a position relate to Parliamentary accountability? How much would it cost? Nevertheless the independent Chief Inspector, whose creation was resisted so fiercely with the same arguments, recommended the establishment of a prisons ombudsman.

This then is the prison system in Britain – overcrowded, desperately seeking to survive from day to day, without a rationale with which to motivate its employees or a minimum level of constructive occupation to offer many of its residents, arbitrary and oppressive in the operation of its rules, and deeply resistant to independent scrutiny.

Chapter 3
What Needs to be Done to Reduce the Use of Prison?

'BANG UP YOBS' CALL

There's only one answer to drunken yobs who beat up coppers, the Police Federation said yesterday: Forget community service and bang them up. Federation spokesman Tony Judge said: "The time has come to say No to pleas for some 'poor little bugger' not to be locked up.

"The truth is that punishment like community service doesn't work in many cases. Courts must be tougher.

"There is only one answer to yobs who assault officers – bang them up. It is the only language they know." The federation claims that assaults on officers now run at 15,000 a year.

Mr Judge said: "It has become a major problem. Anywhere a policeman attempts to enforce the law he is likely to be assaulted.

(*Daily Mirror* 24 March 1988)

The prison system must be reformed, because it is wasteful and unjust. But prisons are part of a wider spectrum. They are at the end of a long process. Environments are created where all the elements – poverty, unemployment, decaying housing, the destruction of living communities – breed crime. Crimes are committed against those who are the most vulnerable. They are dealt with by policing that is not very effective. Some offenders are caught. Eventually they come to court. Through a fairly chancy process some end up in prison.

The pathway to the prison system leads through a tangle of injustice, and highlights particularly sharply the acceptance of enormous inequalities, the readiness to punish the poor for their poverty, so characteristic of our social arrangements. The prison system is not as it is just through mischance and neglect, though they have played their part. It is also as it is because it reflects beliefs and satisfies a deep hunger to see others punished.

Prison reform and crime policy

To consider its reform in isolation would be both wrong and politically impractical. There are many other wrongs that anyone responsible for crime policy would wish to ameliorate. Crime policy has to be reformulated as a whole. Prison reform can be but part of such a reorientation. It is unfair that women feel imprisoned in their homes and unable to go out at night, through fear of being molested or attacked. It is unjust that black families feel they cannot move to a better home for fear of being harassed, abused, subjected to racial taunts and insults and eventually driven out by racist white neighbours. It is unacceptable for old people already living in poverty to have to barricade themselves behind a bristling array of locked bolts to protect their meagre pension money and few possessions from local burglars.

Prisons policy must therefore be part of a wider crime policy. And a wider crime policy must take into account the two faces of crime – the myths and the facts. The facts are imperfectly known. They are that breaking the law is a very widespread and commonplace activity. In 1987, 3.9 million notifiable offences i.e. excluding less serious traffic offences, were recorded by the police. Not all offences are reported to the police or recorded by them. Many people do not bother to report minor offences because they think it is not worth it – or would rather keep the police out of it. Offences where there is no obvious victim, for example damage to public property, are only recorded if a police officer notices and decides to record them. Research suggests that the reported figure represents about a fifth of all offences actually committed – so there may be up to 20 million offences committed annually.

Many people break the law. Thirty per cent of men have a criminal conviction for a notifiable offence by their twenty-eighth birthday. Lawbreaking is well spread through all social groups, though the way it manifests itself differs according to the opportunities presented by the environment, and the way it is prosecuted and punished varies with the social status of those engaging in it. Thus, people with access to enormous amounts of money in the City may be tempted to indulge in various forms of fraud. People in work who are less than honest steal from their employers. A study carried out in 1986 found that commercial fraud recorded by London Fraud Squads represents almost three times the total cost of all other property crime in London. Many serious frauds were unrecognised by the victims or unreported. Fiddling of expenses, income tax or VAT is widespread. Men in all social classes are violent to their wives and children. People out of work who are tempted to transgress may steal from others in the neighbourhood. Young people who are going through a rebellious phase treat their surroundings as an adventure playground, experiment with drugs or take and drive away cars. Women who are bringing up children on their own on a very low income, and decide they can no longer manage may fail to pay their TV licence or may defraud the social security.

Most crimes are against property. Crimes against people cause more concern. Out of the 3.9 million crimes recorded in 1987, just under 200,000, or 5 per cent, were crimes against the person. 7,000 were trafficking in controlled drugs and 1,900 were serious offences against public order.

The statistical chances of being a victim of violence are not great. Because of the large number of unreported crimes, the best estimates of how many people have been victims of crime come from large-scale surveys. The Home Office's British Crime Survey is based on a representative sample of 11,000 people in England and Wales. The results suggest that statistically the average person aged sixteen or over in 1981 could expect to suffer a robbery, i.e. theft accompanied by violence, every five centuries and an assault resulting in injury every 100 years.

The chances of being a victim of any crime at all are not as great as is generally believed. A survey conducted by MORI in November 1987 showed that 56 per cent of the sample interviewed had never contacted the police about a crime and 60 per cent had never suffered any violent crime, a burglary, theft or criminal damage.

However, there is no doubt that the 40 per cent who have been victims of crime are not spread evenly throughout the country. The crimes about which people are personally most concerned, burglary and assault, occur disproportionately in poor urban areas, on housing estates, against people least able to protect themselves with security devices or insurance cover. The British Crime Survey showed that if you live in the inner city your chances of being burgled are twice that of those living in other built-up areas and five times higher than the chances of those living in the country. Victims of crime are more likely to live in urban areas, rented accommodation, flats – and to be young, single men. A study in Liverpool showed that three in a hundred of the people living in an affluent suburb had suffered a burglary or attempted burglary in one year. The figure for a poor inner city district was one in four.

These then are the facts. Crime is widespread and commonplace, not committed by exceptional and depraved people but by next-door neighbours and work colleagues. Violent crime (though increasing) is still very rare. Most people (six out of ten) say they have never been a victim of assault or theft. Compared with other European countries, our dishonesty rate is relatively high, our car theft rate is the highest, but our serious violence rate is comparatively low.

These facts are of very little interest to the crime reporters and editors of most newspapers. The myths are more exciting. Crime is threatening to engulf us all. Violence lurks round every corner. Crime is perpetrated by special, different, fear-inducing people (here a hint of racism often creeps in) who have to be tracked down and locked away for a long time. The case of the Neighbourhood Watch leaflet put out by Staffordshire police which asked for "sightings of coloureds and their vehicle numbers" in order to prevent crime is not an isolated aberration. The notion of a criminal class, though there is no Australia to which to banish it, still lingers. Television programmes about crime, even the responsible, serious ones, have to be attention-grabbing and entertaining. The BBC's Crimewatch programme is unlikely to start off, after the arresting introductory music, by saying "It's been a very peaceful week. Many thousands of banks and building societies conducted millions of transactions with their customers without any act of violence taking place or being threatened. In 99 per cent of Britain's villages and small towns no assaults took place; 99 per cent of the old age pensioners who went to a place of entertainment after 6pm got home safely. This is the context in which we present to you this week the three violent and appalling crimes that did take place that we want your help with."

The tabloids are not likely to do centre-page spreads called "Peaceful Britain" rather than the recurring features on violent Britain with enlargements of often-used photographs of elderly women with horrific injuries.

Crime policy must take account of the facts. But it also cannot ignore the myths. It has to start therefore from the position that most people quite reasonably want something to be done about crime. And in the absence of any other suggestions they may well see more and more prisons as an answer.

Doing something about crime is increasingly recognised as important. In the 1983 General Election campaign the Labour Party put together an entirely new policy on the theme of crime prevention, promising crime prevention grants for installing stronger locks, better doors and vandal-proof glass, better street lighting, more caretakers, security patrols and park wardens and a safer design for housing estates. The Conservative Government is making a major feature of its crime prevention programme with a large budget for whole page advertisements in newspapers, on hoardings, television commercials and a glossy booklet "Let's Crack Crime". And it is not all just publicity. Crime prevention schemes, under the heading "Safer Cities", have been launched in various urban centres and a new organisation, "Crime Concern", to carry forward the crime prevention message outside Government, is operating across the country.

Well-publicised crime prevention programmes are increasingly seen as an important part of any government's crime policy. In France a national strategy of juvenile crime prevention has been the main feature of juvenile crime control. Following inner city disturbances in 1981, the socialist government set up an interdepartmental commission to study the problem of French youth. The outcome was a three-tier system of crime prevention committees involving central and local government and voluntary organisations. The third tier committees at local level organise a range of activities aimed at the young. By 1983 two thirds of towns and cities with over 30,000 inhabitants had such a committee.

Crime prevention though can come in various forms, according to the philosophy of those who promote it. One view of crime prevention would equip every home that had worldly goods worth speaking of with status-symbol crime prevention hardware – burglar alarms, window locks, front door bolts and chains, a dog perhaps, or a high-tech machine that makes a dogbarking noise when an intruder passes near it. Those with large amounts of worldly goods might even feel safer living in 'a development' with a guard at the entrance and, to prevent unauthorised entry, a range of security devices of the sort normally used in prisons to prevent unauthorised exit. Those running public services such as transport systems might, in the spirit of the age, carry out their cost-cutting and replace staff by machines; then, when people stop using their tube trains because the deserted stations and platforms have become frightening places, install video cameras so an official can sit in a control room watching what goes on.

Such a form of crime prevention, taken to its conclusion, leads to a hideous vision of the 'haves' living in fortified condominiums with narrow, guarded entrances, whilst the 'have-nots' hover outside the barbed wire, looking for a chance to evade the numerous security guards and ever-increasing police forces, and get inside to grab something.

A different approach to crime prevention takes a wider view. It is not enough to put in a new front door for the housing estate resident who has had the front door kicked in six times. It is also necessary to ask "What else is there for teenagers to do on this estate but kick doors in?", and then start providing something. Cost-cutting measures such as reducing the numbers of caretakers do not cut costs if vandalism goes up, lifts have to be constantly repaired, windows mended, rubbish chutes unblocked. A wider view needs to be taken not just of security but of the underlying reasons why a certain housing estate can become a crime-plagued hell for its residents. Elliott Currie, the American criminologist, says of successful crime prevention that it must recognise "that real communities thrive or fail to thrive, become healthy or pathological, mainly as a result of the strength or weakness of these basic institutions – work, family, kin, religious and communal associations, a vibrant local economy capable of generating stable livelihoods".

If the problem of the prisons is to be tackled, therefore, the problem of crime must be tackled. And it has to be understood that the problem of crime is not tackled by the process of catching, trying and sentencing individual criminals. The problem of crime will only be dealt with by a different approach to social policies backed up by a specific, substantial, properly funded crime prevention programme. A radical shift in thinking must be made. We must move from seeing the penal system, the courts and the prisons as the main answer to crime, to seeing crime prevention as the main answer to crime. And as thinking moves, so must resourcing.

Within the criminal justice system itself radical shifts must take place, real changes in perception and belief about what the system is for and what it can do. First, one consequence of accepting that the impact of the penal process is very limited is to take steps to use it more sparingly. We must ask the questions, "Why do we prosecute so many people? What is prosecution for? Who benefits from the existing level of prosecution?" Obviously if large numbers of cases were at the level of the one reported in March 1988 where the judge complained bitterly about presiding over a trial costing £3,000 for a theft of a British Rail sandwich from the buffet at Crewe station, the answer would be easy. Presumably, they are not. Even so, since prosecution impinges on a small proportion of the crimes committed annually, it is surely reasonable to reserve it for those which are serious, or which require prosecution for pressing reasons of public policy. In Holland public prosecutors waive about 40 per cent of the cases coming before them and only prosecute when it is "in society's interests". In England and Wales, the Crown Prosecution Service decides whether or not to take a case forward, following guidelines laid down in the Code for Crown Prosecutors. The scope for reducing prosecution is therefore available. It must be used more systematically to divert from court many thousands of minor cases brought against vulnerable people, who may need help from various social agencies but who certainly do not need a day in court and another fine they cannot possibly pay.

A second shift within the criminal justice process must also take place, a shift towards more consideration of victims, up to now a relatively neglected group. Being a victim of crime may impinge very little. It can mean mending one window after a break-in, filling in an insurance form and perhaps ending up with a new piece of equipment to replace an older one which was stolen. Or it can be a traumatic experience which leaves scars for months or years, takes away all self-confidence and leaves the victim facing a restricted lifestyle in an environment that has become terrifying. Proper compensation for victims, either from the offender or from the Criminal Injuries Compensation Board, must be available. Victims' support schemes must be properly funded.

Finally, at the end of the long and chancy process, at the point where a crime has been committed, reported to the police, the right offender has been caught, prosecuted and found guilty, we need yet another radical shift in the process. The time has come to move away from penalties based on imposing suffering as punishment. Penalties must be based on constructive involvement with the community and on reparation. Penalties must be designed to reconcile and re-integrate rather than alienate and embitter. At the very end of the line, where it is inescapable, we need a smaller, less damaging, more constructive prison system.

The idea that a new approach to crime is needed is not going to come as a surprise to most policy-makers. The Home Office attempt to account for itself, "Criminal Justice: A Working Paper", published in 1986, says: "All would agree that the criminal justice system on its own cannot hope to succeed in reversing the upward trend in crime figures. The underlying causes of crime lie within society itself ...".

The messages about crime prevention and about victims have been heard and feature regularly in ministerial utterances. So far, appropriate resourcing lags very far behind. The lion's share of the budget goes to the prisons, around £800 million. Probation comes next with over £230 million. Criminal Injuries Compensation costs just under £70 million. Victims' support gets around £2½ million per year. The Safer Cities scheme and the organisation Crime Concern account for another £2½ million. So the release of some resources for crime prevention and victims has begun. The shift in the penal system away from prison has not. In fact the opposite is happening. The cash expenditure on prisons will nearly double between 1982 and 1990. Running costs per annum must reach a billion before 1990. When the planned growth has taken place, the prison system will not just be the centre of the system. It will have become a gigantic monster, consuming enormous amounts of money every year, sucking in and providing a further education for many thousands of young men who get caught up in petty crime.

This trend must be reversed. Within the context of a crime policy which emphasises crime prevention and gives it the necessary resources, the thinking about prison must be changed. Its place in the gallery of penal sanctions must be changed. The change will be slow and difficult and action will be needed on all fronts simultaneously. The machinery of the penal system will have to be changed to enable policies to be implemented. Legislation will have to be brought in. The way penalties are provided and presented to courts will have to be improved. And a far-reaching debate will have to be launched involving the judiciary, the media and the public.

Relationship between supply and demand

The start must be reducing the use of prison. An attack must be made on the high and unrestrained use of prison – a demand from the courts which it is neither practical nor in the public interest to meet. The UK's high use of prison is bad because it leads to chronic overcrowding, and chronic overcrowding leads to a perpetuation of squalor, permanent crisis management, a failure of planning and the demoralisation of staff. It would be bad even if there were enough room for a single cell for every prisoner and some left over. Penologically, socially and economically, a high use of prison produces no benefits and creates more social problems. Until it is confronted there will always be excuses, partly justified, for not reforming the prison system, for not dealing with the absence of prisoners' rights, the poor regimes, the lack of sentence planning for individual prisoners, the low priority given to staff training and development, the minimal level of community contact and involvement.

At the centre of the problem is a structure which provides no relationship between demand and supply. In few other areas of public life can the consumers of a resource use it freely, with no constraints on its availability, divorced from responsibility for the frequency of its use and awareness of the practical implications. Doctors have to allocate hospital beds in order of priority and establish waiting lists. Universities select from amongst the eligible and eliminate many who want their services. Only judges and magistrates, providing that they keep within legislation and the limits of fairness as set down by the Court of Appeal, have uncontrolled freedom to use their most costly resource, that is, prison, without any accountability for the situation thus created. The individual actions of 150 stipendiary magistrates, 27,700 lay magistrates and 79 High Court Judges, 390 Circuit Judges, 561 Recorders and 471 Assistant Recorders, all acting according to the interests of society as they see it, according to principles of sentencing as taught in their (admittedly brief) training period, all using prison "as a last resort", add up to a prison population, currently of around 50,000.

Sometimes the prison population goes up very quickly. These unexpected surges are analysed afterwards into their component parts, but at the time no one knows whether they will happen, why they are happening and why they are the size they are. So prison administrators watch in despair, helpless to do anything as their statisticians draw them graphs with lines striking ever upwards, widening the gap between accommodation and population still further, suggesting figures that cannot be coped with. The absurdity inherent in this way of doing things prompted a one-time head of the Home Office, Sir Brian Cubbon, admittedly in his last few months in his position and from 15,000 miles away, to ask in a lecture to an Australian Conference: "Will we never find a point of intervention in sentencing decisions themselves? Can we never contemplate inserting mechanisms of 'demand management' into the sentencing process, so that the volume of demand for imprisonment can be more closely tied to the available supply?"

This statement was regarded as newsworthy – daring even, and the fact that it was made prompted reports in the serious newspapers. How is it that such a seemingly innocuous question should be seen as a daring utterance on a taboo subject by a demob-happy civil servant?

Why is it thus? The answer is, because it is constructed like this. A deep divide separates the providers of the resources and the consumers, a divide deeply embedded in the machinery of government and in the consciousness and beliefs of those operating the system. It is the Home Office which is in charge of the resources, the prisons, most of the money for the probation service. It is the Lord Chancellor's Department which regulates the judiciary, and has oversight of the appointment of magistrates.

However, such a divide should not be insuperable. Often ways are found of overcoming unhelpful structures, through joint working arrangements, exerting influence, stimulating internal debate, providing training. In the British system, many seemingly unworkable structures are made to work through informal means. Meetings are held. Joint working methods are agreed. Circulars are issued and implemented. Consultative machinery is established. When we come to the courts, the judiciary, sentencing policy, even these devices become very difficult. A host of assumptions, deep-rooted beliefs about what is right and proper and about who should be allowed to talk to whom, come to the surface and stop progress. The story of the initiative to provide training for judges is illustrative. It arose, in traditional British fashion, from a private meeting held at one of those country houses converted to conference purposes where the great and the good meet to discuss the problems of the age, in this case, at Ditchley Park. All the important people were there, the Home Office, the Lord Chancellor's Department, judges, criminologists, the probation and prison services. At the meeting it was decided that "there was room for improving the transmission of useful information to judges".

The Working Party on Judicial Training and Information was set up in 1975 by the Home Secretary, the Lord Chancellor and the Lord Chief Justice. In 1976 it produced a consultative paper which provoked a hostile reaction in some judicial quarters. According to the final report, the Working Party had to face a "widely felt and strongly voiced objection" to the use of the word "training". The objections were first that the word "training" suggests that there are, somewhere out there, people who can "train" people to be judges. This concept is a threat to judicial independence. Second, people "of the stature and experience to fit them for appointment as judges" will resent the suggestion that they need to be trained. Third, the public will lose confidence in judges if they think they have to be trained before they can judge properly.

The Working Party defends itself against these arguments. They never meant "training" in the sense of indoctrination or conditioning. But they succumbed to the strength of feeling. "Training" had to go. Judicial Studies replaced it and remains as the title.

They also had trouble with the idea, mooted in the 1976 consultative paper, of a three to four week training course for all new judges. The judiciary and the Bar protested strongly. Three to four weeks was too long "for persons of the intellectual calibre of judges, who can be expected to absorb knowledge quickly and to become equally quickly disenchanted with anything less than the best use of their time"; short and intensive periods of study are better. The idea was abandoned.

However, things change. The latest report of the Judicial Studies Board, surveying the achievement of the Board since it was set up in 1979, notes a change of climate: "We doubt whether a change of name to the Judicial 'Training' Board would nowadays raise many eyebrows." Training may now be regarded as less revolutionary. But there is still no agreement that sentencing can be seen much as other aspects of social policy. Research in the Crown Court to find out why judges reach the decisions they do is not allowed. A proposal by the eminently respectable Oxford Centre for Criminological Research to carry out research into sentencing in the Crown Court was turned down by the Lord Chief Justice in 1981. There has been none up to now.

The ideological difficulties are but part of the problem. There are also substantial administrative hurdles to overcome. At least the Crown Courts are under the aegis of the Lord Chancellor's Department with clear lines of accountability. The organisation of the magistrates' courts is so diffuse and obscure as to defy the most determined attempt to structure some accountability and find a point where intervention would be legitimate. The Lord Chancellor's Department is responsible for appointing magistrates. The Home Office is responsible for the administration of magistrates' courts. However, it is more complicated than the simple division between two central government departments. There is also a local structure based on local government boundaries. Thus each county, borough or district has a magistrates' courts committee elected by local magistrates. The committee gets the money for running the court from the local authority. The local authority gets 80 per cent back from the Home Office. The magistrates' courts' committees appoint the local official, the justices' clerk, who runs the court and provides legal advice to the bench. There is also a Council of Magistrates' Courts' Committees.

To introduce any changes of policy into such a system is painful and difficult. To bring about greater effectiveness in collecting fines or scheduling cases, or to ensure implementation of equal opportunities policies in employing court staff, presents major problems. To find a way of starting an educated debate on the use of prison is liable to defeat the most determined.

Structurally the situation is complicated even further by the existence of the Magistrates' Association, a professional body set up to represent magistrates' views and interests and act as a magistrates' pressure group on matters that affect them, such as allowances. Over the years, the Magistrates' Association has emerged as a body with views on sentencing matters against which there is no countervailing point of pressure either from inside Government or outside. In particular they have constituted a powerful lobby for tough measures to be imposed on persistent juvenile offenders. They opposed key elements of the 1969 Children and Young Persons Act and resisted strongly the discretion given to local authorities to decide where to place young people under a care order. They have argued for tougher sanctions for young people failing to keep the conditions of supervision orders and strongly oppose the transfer of jurisdiction over juvenile crime to a family court.

So how does one break into this circle of sentencers, jealously guarding their independence from outside policy making? How can they be brought into a position where questions about their use of resources can be asked? With the points of direct entry thus closed off, efforts to exert influence to, in Sir Brian Cubbon's words, "find a point of intervention in sentencing decisions themselves" have therefore been oblique. They have been concentrated on the least controversial and most politically marketable strategy, that is, to create other punishments, other forms of disposing of convicted offenders, and then try to persuade the judges and magistrates to use them more and to use prison less. Hence these measures have very unhelpfully come to be called alternatives to prison.

Alternatives to prison

Such a strategy has been pursued since 1967. In that year the Criminal Justice Act brought in suspended prison sentences. This provided for the sentence to be imposed – with all the implications such as a criminal record – but not to be served. The sentence would only be activated if the offender came back to court for committing another crime. In 1972 a further Criminal Justice Act brought in community service orders. After an experimental start in six areas, these orders – which require offenders to do up to 240 hours of work of benefit to the community in their free time – were introduced in 1975 and 1976. The 1982 Criminal Justice Act brought in two more possibilities. First there were to be partly suspended sentences. Second, a power was created to require someone to spend up to sixty days at a probation day centre as a condition of a probation order. This strategy of bringing in new measures has been accompanied by constant exhortations to the judiciary to use prison less and to use these other disposals more.

Unfortunately this strategy has failed. It is now a widely accepted view that suspended sentences, for instance, far from reducing the use of prison, have in fact increased it. This is because the courts have in some cases imposed a suspended sentence on people who would otherwise not have got a prison sentence at all or imposed a much longer suspended sentence than a non-suspended one would have been. Some of these people commit further crimes. They then end up in prison serving an activated suspended sentence as well as possibly a prison sentence for the second offence.

Community service orders and the various stiffened forms of probation have not made dramatic inroads into the use of prison. They may well have helped at the margins but overall their effect seems to have been to take offenders away from other non-custodial penalties. The figures make this clear. Between 1977 and 1986 the proportion of offenders sentenced for indictable offences who went straight to prison rose from 13 per cent to 18 per cent. The use of probation and community service together increased by 10 per cent and the proportion of those fined fell from 51 per cent in 1977 to 38 per cent in 1987. Overall therefore there has been a shift. Prison is used more. Probation and community service are used more. The fine is used much less. The reasons for this change of habit amongst the judiciary are not hard to establish. During those years unemployment increased substantially and many of those coming before the courts did not have the money to pay the kind of financial penalty that many courts regard as necessary, because they have no way of systematically relating levels of fines to people's means.

It is clear, if unfortunate, that the strategy of attempting to make inroads into the proportionate use of prison by establishing other penalties and hoping that by some unexplained logic the courts would feel moved to change their habits has not been successful. It must have seemed quite disappointing to the successive Home Secretaries who pursued this path that having explained to courts that prison was ineffective, very expensive and incidentally very overcrowded, having got through Parliament legislation for so many other options, no one seemed to be very responsive. It may be some consolation to them that this disappointing outcome is not restricted to this country. The Canadian Sentencing Commission notes:

> The rationale for introducing a number of programs has been to reduce the number of offenders incarcerated and thereby relieve prison overcrowding. It is now becoming increasingly apparent that community sanctions do not in fact currently have this effect. Studies in different jurisdictions have indicated that while the number of individuals being sent to prison has either remained unchanged or has increased, the numbers admitted to community programs has steadily increased.

The question has to be asked, "why is this the way it works?" Undoubtedly a combination of factors is to blame. First the strategy has been pursued in a way that has always left the advantage with prison in the minds of judges and magistrates. The strategy has always accepted the assumptions of the whole "alternatives to prison" debate in which, as the Canadian Sentencing Commission describes it, imprisonment is "viewed as the pivotal sanction with all other dispositions considered as forms of leniency".

The supply of prison has always been regarded as unlimited. Whenever there is a crisis in which demand outstrips supply, the consequences have not fallen on the courts. They have fallen on the prison service. No one says to the courts (except perhaps in the celebrated instance of 1981 when the prison officers took industrial action), "You have got to cut down on your use of prison. There is a crisis. If you do not restrain your use voluntarily a limit will have to be imposed." Certainly no one seriously considers the Dutch solutions: for sentenced prisoners set up a waiting list; for unsentenced prisoners send home the one least needing a remand place to make room for the one that does. What happens is that the prison service is sent off hunting down disused buildings, measuring up workshops for dormitories, distributing campbeds, finding police forces prepared to allow the use of their police cells and coping somehow.

As far as the sentencers are concerned therefore, prison is infinitely elastic. The more they use the more there will be. Compare this with the way community service orders are provided. Community service is run by the probation service and comes out of a fixed budget. Only so many places are budgeted for. These places can run out. Sometimes they do. So courts can be told that community service is full and they will have to wait for a vacancy and use something else in the meantime. Community service and probation orders have "gatekeepers", in the sense that they are not usually imposed without the providers, that is the probation service, having done an investigation and recommended that they would be workable and advantageous.

Second, the structural difference between the way prison is provided and the way community service and probation orders are provided puts the non-custodial penalties at a disadvantage. Prisons are part of a national system, run according to national rules. After a few visits to prison the sentencers can be reasonably sure they know the framework of the punishment they are imposing. They are probably shielded from the sight and smell of slopping out at 7am or the wails and groans of the mentally ill people in the prison hospital. Nevertheless, they can take away with them the picture of a prison officer in a uniform with peaked cap, a rule book, a disciplinary system, small cells, jangling keys, an institutional routine, an image of prison life which will fit reasonably well with what happens to those they send to prison. On the other hand, the non-custodial penalties, probation orders and community service orders, are provided locally by fifty-six different probation services with different approaches, priorities, attitudes and styles. In some areas, relationships between the probation service and the judiciary may be good, and may be founded on mutual respect; in others they may be characterised by suspicion, mistrust and a profound ideological divide.

The third reason why the "alternatives to custody" strategy has failed is the lack of clarity with which the "alternatives" have been introduced. The way they have been launched upon the sentencing world has maximised debate and confusion about their use and further detracts from their attraction when compared with, say, "three months" or "six months". There are very few judicial pronouncements about their use in the way that there are on matters such as the appropriate sentences for rape, for instance. A bench of magistrates in one geographical location can decide that in their court community service orders will only be used when the magistrates have decided that otherwise the offender would go to prison. In the next court, just down the road, the magistrates can decide that community service is a very useful penalty for a whole range of offenders, from those who might otherwise go to prison to those who have been unemployed for a long time and might benefit from a chance to do some worthwhile voluntary work. Such lack of clarity leaves room for so much discretion that the objective of reducing the use of custody is rapidly lost. Further complications arise when an offender doing community service breaks the conditions and is brought back to court. If the order was genuinely imposed instead of prison, then the court hearing the breach of conditions could reasonably say prison is appropriate. But suppose the order had been imposed when prison was not in question, what then? The original court might know. The court hearing the breach might not. Not only an increase in the prison population but an injustice might well result.

Finally, the main non-custodial penalty which has perhaps the greatest potential to reduce the use of custody, that is, the community service order, is run by a social work agency, the probation service. This adds a further confusion. Perceptions that community service should be therapeutic or rehabilitative bump up against the search by the courts for something simple, uniformly provided and punitive.

So, substantial structural barriers stand in the way of a more rational, cost-effective sentencing policy, and a more rational sentencing policy is the key to a more sparing use of prison. Until the over-use of prison is tackled, the system will be continually swamped by population crises and at the mercy of quite unpredictable demands. The energy needed to improve the system itself will always be diverted to managing the crisis and overcrowding will be the justification for low standards and barren regimes.

Changing sentencing practice

However, it would be wise not to underestimate the tremendous size of the obstacles that block the path to a reduced use of prison by the courts. One thing reassures. Almost everyone who has pondered the matter, when asked "What would you see as the great obstacle to reforming the prisons?" would say "the high use of prison by the courts". The unanimity is striking. But with the next question it all becomes much harder. The unanimity dissipates. When asked "How would you tackle the high use of prison by the courts?" two classes of respondents will emerge. One group, suffering from deep-rooted pessimism, will say that it cannot be done, that every device within current constitutional bounds has been discussed, tried, failed or been rejected as unacceptable to the judiciary. There are no policy options available that are politically acceptable.

The other group of respondents will reply in a way that divides them quickly into entrenched camps. There is the "legislation-is-the-only-way" school. They argue that courts are subject to the will of Parliament and it is up to Parliament to pass laws lowering maximum penalties. If Parliament did so, the courts, having been given a clear indication of the will of Parliament, would respond.

The sceptics argue back. First, they say that it is not politically realistic to expect such legislation to get through Parliament. It is not feasible for any party. Look what happened when the Advisory Council on the Penal System, a think tank set up in 1966 by Roy Jenkins, produced a report in 1978 arguing very carefully and rationally for a reduction in maximum sentences whilst allowing higher sentences than the maximum to be passed in exceptional circumstances. There was uproar. The Labour Government of the time dropped the report like a hot potato. It was never implemented, or even properly discussed.

Second, they say that legislation cannot eliminate discretion. Maximum penalties are already so high in relation to the average sentence length. Fourteen years in prison is the maximum for burglary. In 1986 only 30 per cent of burglars got an immediate prison sentence. More than half of them were sentenced to eighteen months or less. It is suggested therefore that lowering the maximum will not make a lot of difference to what the courts actually do.

Another branch of the legislation-is-the-only-way school advocates using it in a different way, to tighten up the rules surrounding the use of custody, to make the courts go through a series of stages and satisfy a number of criteria before imposing custody. These enthusiasts point to the impact of the 1976 Bail Act which set out the conditions for withholding bail. In 1975, over 68,000 people were remanded in custody. In 1978 the figure had dropped to 52,500. By 1986 it had reached 63,500, still lower than the pre Bail Act figure and proportionately about the same as in 1978. These enthusiasts also claim that Section 1(4) of the 1982 Criminal Justice Act, laying down criteria for consideration before sending young people to prison, has been successful, though sceptics argue that the evidence is ambiguous.

On the same track, but with a more complex approach, is the "sorting out sentencing policy" school. They argue that the judiciary will never accept interference from outside but might be prepared to do some restructuring themselves. The judiciary should therefore draw up guidelines themselves, more coherent than the decisions made by the Court of Appeal, setting out clearly the circumstances in which particular sentences should be given. The hope behind this is that introducing more logic and structure into sentencing will lead to a reduction in the use of prison. Unfortunately, this only seems to work if those producing the guidelines think it logical to reduce the use of prison. The sentencing guidelines pattern is now operating in some American states, where it seems that the development of sentencing guidelines has contributed to an increase in the use of imprisonment and an increase in the length of prison sentences. An interesting variation in Minnesota is more successful. There, the Sentencing Commission adjusts the guidelines periodically to maintain a fairly stable prison population.

The Minnesota system of guidelines exemplifies the thinking of the "rationing" school. Rationing is a very tempting proposition, with a nice parallel with the cash limits so many public sector bodies now have to keep within. The supporters of rationing suggest that courts should be given a finite amount of prison, say so many person-months, based on an analysis of current patterns. It would then be up to them to decide how to use their allocation. The next step would be for the allocation to be gradually scaled down each year until it reached a much lower level of use of prison than we have now. The concept bubbles up whenever reducing the use of prison is on the agenda, although the idea has never been developed beyond the stage where the questions are asked, "suppose you run out of prison months before the end of the year, what then?", or "suppose you have got a lot of unused months left at the year end. It would be bad luck for the defendant appearing then". Everyone smiles, and rationing sinks back into the realms of the totally impractical. The lesson of Minnesota, that sentencing guidelines which command agreement can be drawn up and can be adjusted in the light of sentencing practice, is too radical to accept.

Another group would put their emphasis on changing the structure and could be called the structural school. They would say that nothing can really happen until something is done to clarify the practical working meaning of the division between the executive and the judiciary. A definition of what relationship is constitutional and what boundaries cannot be crossed is essential. What the independence of the judiciary really means needs to be pinned down. A recurring lack of clarity about what is interference in individual cases and what is proper policy-making about the shape, emphasis and resourcing of the penal system must be resolved. Only then can productive discussions about policy take place. Presumably there are already meetings between the Home Secretary and the Lord Chancellor and the Lord Chief Justice to discuss matters of mutual interest. Presumably also at such meetings, the Home Secretary discusses the state of the prisons, the accumulated evidence of the ineffectiveness of prison, the high use of prison, the enormous cost of going on like this and the need for change. He may even dare to come down to pounds and pence and mention, as if in passing, that a prison place costs £252 a week to run, whereas a week's probation costs £15 and week's community service under £13. Even a residential place in a probation hostel is only £155.

The other two then presumably look sympathetic and understanding but make the point most politely that justice cannot be cash-limited. It will be a sad day, they murmur, when a judge does not what is right but what will keep the system within its budget. Presumably then the Lord Chancellor goes on to say how sorry he is about the Home Secretary's predicament. He sympathises greatly and he wishes he could help. He himself would really like to reduce the use of prison too. But of course, it is up to the judges. They both then turn to the Lord Chief Justice who says, one imagines, he too is sorry but it is not really his business. Judges are independent. The law gives them the freedom to choose a sentence from within a range. There is a lot of pressure from public opinion for longer and longer sentences. Considering such pressure they really are doing quite well to keep the prison population to the level it is. The Home Secretary then smiles weakly at the thought that it could all be even worse. Then the ministerial cars come and they all glide away, back to their separate offices, no further forward.

Mechanisms need to be found to bring the various parts of the process together so that those who provide the resources can talk to those who use them, so that there can be, running across all the parts of the system, something recognisable as 'a penal policy'. Various suggestions have been made as to how this could be done. In 1981 the Home Affairs Select Committee published a report on the prison service. The Committee considered, as have committees before and since, the obstinate problem of the overuse of prison. It linked the problem to structural gaps in the system and pointed out how greatly we suffer from the fragmentation of criminal policy-making in this country. It went on to recommend the establishment of a National Criminal Policy Committee with a brief to construct a comprehensive criminal justice policy. The membership, the Committee suggested, should be drawn from the Home Office, Lord Chancellor's Department, DHSS, senior judiciary, magistracy, police, probation service and local authorities.

Another idea for a new structure, complementary rather than contradictory, is that of a Sentencing Council, first proposed by the influential academic lawyer Andrew Ashworth in 1982. Such a council would have as members experienced magistrates and judges, with input from the probation and prison services and academics. It would need a properly resourced secretariat and could begin the long and arduous process of introducing some logic into a sentencing system widely regarded as illogical, confusing and unfair.

A third structural proposal is more fundamental. That is the proposal for really radical change, for creating a Ministry of Justice. The idea is not new, but has never progressed beyond the discussion stage. It is widely agreed that the present allocation of responsibilities between the Lord Chancellor's Department, Home Office and Attorney General is nonsensical. Comparisons with other Western European countries are difficult because the legal systems are very different. However, in many Western countries the criminal justice system is dealt with by one Ministry. Many functions which in England and Wales come under the Home Office come under a separate Ministry of the Interior. Comparable countries with a Ministry of Justice take the independence of the judiciary as seriously as it is taken in Britain. Nevertheless it has proved possible for some of these Ministries to develop policies on matters such as judicial training or the use of imprisonment, and implement their policies. The idea of a Ministry of Justice attracts many in Britain who want to see reform. However, a sceptic could argue that simply putting all the elements under one roof will not make any difference unless all the parties really want anything to change. If they really want anything to change there is no need to wait for such a major upheaval as creating a new Ministry. Change could happen straight away.

Early release from prison

All these arguments – rationing, legislation, structural change – are looking at the front end, that is, how to stop the courts sending more people to prison in the first place. A whole range of ideas and devices can be produced to reduce the number of prisoners at the other end, that is, once they have been sent to prison. In other countries some novel practices have been developed. In Holland for instance, there is a call-up system. If there is not enough prison space, people given a prison sentence who were not kept in custody before their trial, and presumably are not therefore a danger to the community, are put on a waiting list. When their turn comes, they get a letter telling them to turn up at a semi-open prison, as the Dutch call them, to serve their sentences. One of the numerous reports on prisons, the report of the Home Affairs Committee published in 1981, recommended such an experiment be tried in this country. But as with almost all the recommendations made about prisons by official committees, the idea was completely rejected.

Another device is the system used in Ireland, where periodically the Government releases a number of prisoners to bring the population down to a manageable level. A similar thought prompted the power given to the Home Secretary in the 1982 Criminal Justice Act, to release prisoners in an emergency in the last six months of their sentence. The power has never been used.

The remission of some part of the sentence as a reward for good behaviour is common in many countries and is an obvious device to have in places like prisons where people are kept against their will and need to see very good reasons to put up with the deprivations they are enduring. The chance to get out early is clearly a very good reason to keep quiet and behave reasonably well. Remission, though, has other uses. It can be tinkered with to reduce the numbers locked up. This is the measure Douglas Hurd resorted to in his first crisis, July 1987, when he increased remission from one third to one half on sentences of one year or less. The population was reduced by 3,000, though, not surprisingly, it climbed up again very quickly and was at the same level six months later.

Parole is another letting-out mechanism that has considerable potential. Leon Brittan used this in his first few months as Home Secretary. At the Conservative Party Conference in October 1983, he announced an extension of parole to short-term prisoners so that anyone serving ten and a half months or more would be eligible for release on parole after one third of the sentence. This reduction at the lower end was unfortunately balanced by increased harshness at the top end. No one sentenced to more than five years for an offence involving violence or drug trafficking would get parole at all, except in "wholly exceptional" circumstances or at the very end of the sentence. The immediate effects were a reduction at the lower end of about 2,000 and an increase at the upper end of 500 prisoners.

A bolder proposal for using the parole system to reduce the population is the idea of a supervised release scheme, whereby all those serving three years or less would automatically be released after one third to serve the second third outside but under supervision. First floated by the Home Office itself in 1981 it gathered some support – though the judiciary did not like it at all. However, it was not the judiciary that dealt the death blow. It was the Conservative Party Conference. It was the 1981 Conference where William Whitelaw was publicly humiliated and had his law and order motion defeated. Shortly afterwards, the proposal was quietly dropped. It would have reduced the prison population by 7,000.

The trouble with these devices for letting people out – parole, remission – is that if there are a lot of them, with different rules for those serving different sentence lengths, the outcome is chaotic. The effect of Leon Brittan's changes was to make the judges very restless and lead them to protest at what they saw as the erosion of their decisions. There have also been strong protests about the elimination of differentials in sentencing and the flattening of most eighteen-month sentences to a minimum six months. Judge Finney, one of a number of judges who have publicly voiced concern, wrote to *The Times* about the outcome of a hypothetical case of four young men aged 17–22, all involved in robbing a shop and all displaying different degrees of culpability. The judge gives the seventeen-year-old twelve months (he was the look-out) the eighteen- and twenty-year-olds fifteen and eighteen months respectively and the twenty-two-year-old ring leader two years. If the maximum possible parole is given the three youngest could be released in six months and the twenty-two-year-old in eight months.

In response to these concerns, Douglas Hurd set up a committee under Lord Carlisle to look into the parole system and come up with some proposals on whether it should continue, and if so what it should be for and how it should work. They were also asked to consider either changes in the current system or introducing a new system, and in particular whether prisoners released before the end of their sentence should be doing some community work.

Parole and remission are not quite the only letting-people-out mechanisms. Allowing prison authorities some discretion in how prisoners serve their sentence is well developed in some other countries. In the Canadian Federal system, for instance, which takes all prisoners in Canada serving more than two years, quite large proportions of short-term prisoners serve part of their sentence on leave from prison in a hostel of some sort, undergoing what across the Atlantic is called "a programme" of education or training of some sort. In Sweden, drug-abusing prisoners may choose to serve part of their sentence living with a family in a rural area, far from the temptations of the city life, providing they accept a commitment to remain drug-free. Apart from a very limited pre-release employment scheme and some opportunities for day parole and home leave, such developments have never been a major part of the scene in Britain.

Local action to change sentencing

The proponents of all these solutions have been arguing their cases for some years. More recently, a new set of arguments has emerged, which could loosely be called the cultural-procedural or "local action" school. Their arguments start not from an overall national policy on sentencing, nor from post-sentence tinkering. They begin in the courtroom, and focus on each individual sentencing decision. And they ask the question, why have the initiatives taken at central Government level, for example the creation of community penalties to be used instead of prison, been so ineffective? They would see the lesson of the past few years as that, even when there has been agreement on a policy to follow and this has been enshrined in legislation, it does not work out in the average courtroom as envisaged by the legislators.

The local action enthusiasts therefore start by analysing how a sentencing decision is made. They look at the inputs to the court, the advice it is given and, for the magistrates' court, the culture of the court. Something, they argue, must account for the gross discrepancies in sentencing in magistrates' courts. There must be a reason why, as one Home Office research study found, 7 per cent of burglars coming up in one court are sent to prison compared with 47 per cent in another, why 48 per cent of first offenders caught shoplifting are fined in one court, compared with 86 per cent in another. The reason is the sentencing culture of the court, and this derives from the ethos set by the leading magistrates in the area handed down by local tradition over many years, and from the influence of the justices' clerk. The justices' clerk controls the training given to the magistrates and gives them advice on the law. Part of the culture of the court is the attitude it has to probation officers. When probation officers write a report on an offender and make a recommendation for, say, a probation order, the courts can be very impressed and take the suggestion seriously. Or they can have a view that the probation service is a bunch of softies that is always on the side of the criminal – and not take the suggestion seriously at all. The priority the probation service gives to its reports for the courts, and to showing magistrates how good its work is, can also vary very much from one area to another. Also a court may not have the slightest idea that it is using prison frequently compared with the court in the next town. Magistrates do not as a matter of course look at figures for their sentencing performance in a given year and compare them, to be surprised at them, analyse them or decide to change their practices.

This lack of any coherence, planning or feedback is the basis of the proposals of the local action school. They advocate working with each bench of magistrates, first to analyse what they are doing, then to tell them what they are doing and finally to organise ways of persuading them to change what they are doing.

The strength of the local action school is their argument that their method has been proved to work. In 1983 the Department of Health and Social Security, which is responsible for overall policy on juvenile crime (juveniles are those aged ten to sixteen), took a major initiative. After years of concern about the very high numbers of fourteen–sixteen-year-olds locked up in prison establishments, and the failure of exhortations to courts not to lock up so many, the DHSS decided on more active intervention. Money was provided for any voluntary group that could set up a local scheme providing an alternative programme for juveniles. The conditions were that the scheme had to be run jointly by all the interested parties, including the police and the magistrates, and that it had to be targeted. No one would get the money to keep 200 youngsters out of detention centres when in their own area no more than twenty a year ever went there. Nor could the schemes just sit and wait for the young people to be sent to them. They had to work with the courts to identify the right ones, make sure the courts knew what would happen on the scheme and keep the court informed of the young person's progress.

The initiative is regarded as a success. In 1983, 6,800 fourteen- to sixteen-year-olds were locked up. In 1987 the figure was 4,000. Some of the reduction is due to demographic change. Most of it is not.

The enthusiasts say this method should be applied to the rest of the work of the courts, particularly to the next age-group, that is the seventeen–twenty-year-olds, who also have a slightly different sentencing system from adults. The sceptics urge caution. Even if the method is accepted and extended to the rest of the magistrates' courts, it will not have overmuch effect. The vast proportion of prison-years are consumed by the judges sitting in the Crown Court. Although magistrates account for a large proportion of those sent to prison – 51 per cent if fine defaulters are included – the sentences they can give are much shorter. The length of the average prison sentence given by a magistrates' court in 1986 was 2.8 months; 85 per cent of the average daily prison population has found its way there from the Crown Court, where the average length of sentence given in 1986 was 18.0 months, having risen from 16.4 months in 1983.

The search for the harsh alternative

Looking back, the discussions on how to reduce the prison population have gone round and round the same circle. The same proposals have been aired at numerous conferences and seminars and had the same cold water poured on them. Each new Government has had representations made to it. All the old ideas have been dusted off by the civil servants and by the various groups. Governments have tried a little bit of this and a little bit of that – remission increased here, parole extended there. They have tried with legislation such as Section 1(4) of the Criminal Justice Act. They have talked to the probation service about being more focused and having objectives. They have given some tiny grants to some voluntary organisations for a few projects.

All this activity has had some effect. The Home Office's annual publication of doom, the statistical bulletin on projections of long-term trends in the prison population, says of the tinkerings just listed, "Most of these changes restrained the increase in the prison population". And restrain it they did, up to 1984. So when the mood changed with Leon Brittan as Home Secretary the increases were dramatic. However, even with a restrained increase the prognosis is very gloomy.

And gloom can lead down some dangerous paths. One idea that regularly surfaces is the search for the harsh alternative. The argument runs thus. Prison is used so much and the non-custodial sanctions do not replace it because they are not nasty enough. The courts want to inflict something unpleasant, harsh, clearly punishing. They do not want to have a choice between prison – controlled, disciplined, full of deprivations and humiliations – and probation or community service – run by friendly people not in uniform who try to be helpful, get to know the offender and exert influence to do constructive things. It is not sensible, the courts are believed to be saying, to expect us to make such a choice. We need a real choice between the ultimate deprivation – prison – and a punishment as harsh but without all the cost and the admitted shortcomings of prison – that university of crime and blighter of prospects.

Leon Brittan had a go at finding a harsher alternative in 1984 with the proposal for weekend prison. A Green Paper came out for discussion suggesting that new prison-type places might be set up where offenders could be sent at weekends or for day attendance. The idea did not survive very long against the combined onslaughts of practically all those consulted. It also began to look rather expensive.

But the search for the harsh alternative does not go away. Once again it is current, this time centred on the efforts of certain electronics companies to sell some devices they have developed which can be strapped to parts of people and when activated can tell a controller where they are. Electronic tagging, as it is called, has so far been used only in North America.

The seminal project seems to have been in Palm Beach Courts, Florida, which introduced an "In-House Arrest System" in December 1984 for offenders on probation and for prisoners on work-release from the local minimum-security prison. The probationers scheme was run by a non-profit private corporation called Pride Inc. The costs of running the corporation are met in part by charging those being supervised by it. Fifteen sets of electronic equipment were available and drunk-driving offenders were offered a choice of thirty days on the electronic equipment or ten days in gaol. If they chose the thirty days on the equipment they had to fulfil certain conditions, namely to pay Pride Inc. about $60 a week, install a telephone if they did not have one, or move in with a friend who did, stay in during the hours of curfew, and report weekly to the probation office to have the tag inspected, pay the fees and discuss any problems. Every weekday morning the probation officer looked at a printout from the computer on each probationer's movements.

Apart from the many civil liberties objections to electronic tagging in itself, there are also many more general arguments against going down the path of trying to solve prison overcrowding by inventing a prison-like punishment that does not have the disadvantages of prison. First, any new punishment would not replace prison. It would replace other non-prison punishment. All the evidence shows that most courts will not resist the temptation to use a new non-custodial penalty, especially a seemingly tough one, to replace existing less tough options. A new order incorporating electronic surveillance would be used mainly instead of probation and community service. If it were widely used, community service orders would become the standard low-level non-custodial penalty for all those who could not pay a fine and the use of prison would continue at its present level.

Second, there are limits as to how much control can realistically be imposed on people. If young men who commit theft are to be confined to their homes between, say, seven in the evening and seven in the morning, additional pressure is put on families living often in the most overcrowded circumstances. The order has to be policed. Resources have to be found to pay those who make random checks. Those who slipped out for a couple of hours to get away from a family row will be discovered, taken back before the bench, and then sent to prison for flouting the wishes of the court. The prison population will then increase even further.

Finally there is no good argument for increasing the amount of punishment available in society. The punishment-hunger of the British psyche requires no further feeding. Instead it must be scaled down, turned in other directions, towards reparative, constructive sanctions which heal and rebuild rather than divide and embitter.

Such propositions must therefore form no part of a strategy to reduce the use of prison. But a strategy there must be.

A strategy for reduction

Reducing the use of prison is going to be a complicated matter calling for action on many fronts. No single decision or line of attack will have much effect on its own. Work will have to be done with many different bodies and agencies, each of which is accountable in a different way, and some of which are only tenuously accountable at all. They all feel the dignity of being part of the criminal justice process and have a strong conviction that their current practice is quite acceptable.

It will be necessary to have a clear view of short-, medium- and long-term objectives. Some changes can start at once. Others require changes in attitude which may take a considerable time to take root. Two decisions, however, must be taken immediately if the current headlong rush in the wrong direction is to be halted. First, a supervised release scheme must be introduced to reduce the prison population at a stroke by 7,000. This can be done without legislation by altering the guidelines for parole to stipulate that prisoners serving under three years should be recommended for full parole other than in "wholly exceptional circumstances". Thus the prison system will be provided with the necessary breathing space to take stock.

A move such as this to reduce the prison population rapidly is an essential basis for the second decision that has to be taken – a decision to freeze the building of all new planned prisons where work has not yet begun. The prison building programme must then be subjected to a detailed analysis based on the questions: is this new prison needed? If so, is it in the right place? Is it the right size? Is its design likely to prove suitable for keeping prisoners in humane and constructive conditions, all with the option of living in a single cell, in the next century? Such a process will reduce the current plans to almost nothing, as those prisons which it could justifiably be argued need to be built as replacements, e.g. Woolwich in London, are much too big at 850 places and contain unacceptable design features such as cells built for double occupation.

Having halted temporarily the process of ever more imprisonment, and ever more building to try and keep pace with it, a number of initiatives have to be taken at once.

A clear and readable document must be produced explaining why it would be socially advantageous to reduce the use of prison in Britain to the level of some of our Western European neighbours and asking for comments and ideas. The document would form the basis of a massive consultation exercise to be undertaken with all interested parties.

A number of other initiatives must be launched very rapidly. A programme like the DHSS scheme for juvenile offenders must be set up to produce similar programmes for 17–20-year-olds. A person must be appointed to each large urban magistrates' court to set up and run a local criminal justice committee. The committee would provide a forum for discussing the work of the court, planning training and identifying the resources the court needs. Notice must be given that custody for 14–16-year-olds will cease to be available within six months, so that alternative arrangements can be made by local authority social services departments.

The closed worlds of decision-makers in the criminal justice process – the judiciary, the civil servants in the Home Office and Lord Chancellor's Department, the power structure in the magistracy – must be opened up to a much wider constituency.

Six task groups of people with expertise must be set up to produce within the year of consultation proposals on certain key areas. Each will canvass a wide range of opinion, commission small-scale studies, compare British experience with what is done in other countries and carry out appropriate well-structured public opinion research. Each should be looking at how the use of prison can be reduced and the criminal justice process be made more effective and more accountable. Public involvement and understanding should be a theme running through each.

The first task group will look at statutory guidelines for sentencers and the experience so far with guidelines for sentencing young offenders and for granting bail. Proposals will then be produced for statutory guidelines to be applied to all decisions to imprison or to refuse bail.

The second, third and fourth groups will look at various non-custodial penalties. One will study community service orders, their use and the confusion surrounding their use. Proposals will be made to restructure community service, give it a clear national profile and clarify the legislation governing it so that it becomes the central and normal sanction for serious property and minor violent crime. The next will consider the scope of the fine and draw up a plan to introduce a new system of fines, so that fines will be fixed appropriately for gravity of offence and then related to ability to pay. The fourth will look at the probation service, its resources, structure, tasks, how compatible they are with each other, and particularly at supervision of offenders in the community, what scope there is for extending it and what facilities are needed to back it up.

A fifth task group will look at the training of judges and magistrates, how it is currently controlled, and develop proposals for broadening its scope and introducing an agreed national training programme on bail and on the effectiveness of sentencing.

The sixth will look at the involvement of the wider community in dealing with offenders, at what services could be provided by the community to defendants coming up in court and to offenders sentenced to non-custodial sanctions, the involvement of volunteers and community organisations with prisons, the need for greater involvement of black people and black community organisations in dealing with offenders and how to achieve it.

All this activity would need to be overseen and co-ordinated. A joint committee would be set up of the Home Secretary, Lord Chancellor, Lord Chief Justice and Attorney General, with a corresponding civil servants' committee. Thus the seeds would be sown of a new structure to bridge the gulf.

The outcome of all the consultations, plans and initiatives should be a new climate. It will then be possible to have a discussion about a different basis of sentencing without cries of "unconstitutional". Good ideas will have had substantial publicity and attracted support. Magistrates' courts will have become more conscious of their overall sentencing patterns and of other ways they could sentence. The time will then be ripe for a major review of sentencing to make sense of the confusion that currently exists. Community sanctions will have become recognised and understood as real penalties to be developed further. A new fining system will be introduced. A more open criminal justice process will allow greater involvement of the wider community with offenders and the penal system. At last, the prison population will stabilise and begin to go down. The population pressure would be off and reform of the prisons can then begin in earnest.

Chapter 4
What Needs to be Done to Reform the Prisons?

> I never saw the moon the whole time I was in Durham. Everyone takes things like that for granted but when you don't see the sky, birds, normal things, animals, trees ... Imagine not seeing a tree for five years or more ... The lights are on in the landings twenty-four hours a day. It's fluorescent lighting; ordinary lighting wouldn't be adequate. The window first had plastic that could open, then you had metal grilles; beyond that you had bars and beyond that there was mesh, and then after that barbed wire. So your only sense when you're buried in that room is your hearing. It was like being buried underground.
>
> (A prisoner speaking of her time at Durham prison from *Insiders: Women's Experience of Prison* by Una Padel and Prue Stevenson)

How to reform the prisons has never provoked the same volume of discussion in Britain as has been generated by arguments on how to reduce imprisonment. Most of the informed debate has concentrated on reducing the population. Once overcrowding has gone and the number of prisoners is reasonably stable, prisons will have got away at last from lurching from crisis to crisis. The rest, it is assumed, will be easy.

However, it would be wise not to underestimate the great distance that has to be travelled from the prison system we have now to a system that incarcerates people *as* and not *for* punishment, a system that respects prisoners' individuality, humanity and dignity. Consider the description given by Michael Ignatieff of how prisoners were received into Pentonville in the 1840s. First they were required to strip naked. Their clothes and possessions were taken away. Then they were required to walk into a bath of disinfectant. After drying, they were inspected by a prison officer and their physical peculiarities were noted in a register. This was followed by a medical inspection by a doctor. Finally, the heads were shaved, the uniforms were issued and the numbers given out.

The prison officers of the 1840s would not find reception procedures in 1988 so different as to be unrecognisable. The rituals that strip away the identity of the individual continue. A woman in her mid-thirties describes to the authors of *Insiders* her arrival on remand at Holloway thus:

> Going through reception they have to check everything you're bringing in, what money you have, or what-have-you. Then they frisk you and give you a dressing gown and tell you to go into a cubicle and strip off and wait. I had to wait a long time shut in. It was a few feet by a few feet with a bench to sit on. After that you go into a big room and they look through your clothes and they ask you questions, then you have to pull your knickers down to your knees and do a twizzle, twist around, pull your pants up and put your dressing gown back on. There were several officers, you felt every eye was on you. It's humiliating, degrading ...

Thus prisoners get the message that they are at the bottom. They have lost their liberty, and much else besides. They are told their rights, but, according to the Chief Inspector, perfunctorily. They are known by a number and addressed by their surname. Men prisoners are put into standard, often ill-fitting prison clothes. They call everyone in authority Sir, Ma'am or Miss or nothing. The uniforms have not changed essentially since the 1840s either. Prison officers wear a uniform in a police/security guard style with an imposing peaked cap, a uniform that, however skilled, professional and caring they are, will always give an impression of the real priorities of the system – security and discipline. It is not inevitably so. In borstals, which were replaced by youth custody centres in 1983, the staff wore civilian clothes. In Holland most prison officers wear civilian clothes, all in the same colours but with no symbols of role or power-relationships.

In prisons in Britain, visitors can come in – magistrates, students, foreign guests – and look at prisoners working, lounging, cleaning, lying in bed sick in a prison hospital, studying. They can peep through spy holes in cell-doors. They are shown cells occupied or unoccupied, covered with pin-ups or family photographs. Prisoners are often discussed with visitors as if they were not there: "He's a bit mentally disturbed, you know." It is not inevitably so. In Sweden, when visitors are going round, an officer precedes and asks the prisoners if they wish to be looked at or to meet visitors. If not they can exercise their right to withdraw out of sight until the visitors have gone.

Also in Sweden, the naive outsider asking to see the visits area and expecting to see a bright, well-decorated room with tables and chairs and a refreshment bar at one end will be surprised. The visits area is a corridor off which lead a number of rooms, like small hotel rooms, each containing a couch, coffee table and chairs. Visits can take place in private for several hours. It is not easy to imagine the British prison system accommodating such arrangements for visits.

In Belgium cells for high-security prisoners are being refurbished. Part of the refurbishment is the installation of a shaver point and a television point in each cell, so that the prisoner's TV can be plugged in. To the Belgian prison governor it seems an obvious thing to do. If people are to lose their liberty and be locked up on their own for hours on end, at least they should be able to watch the television.

The amount of misery locked up behind the walls is difficult to quantify. But there are some indicators. In 1987, thirteen sentenced and twenty-six remand prisoners killed themselves in prison. In 1986/87 occurred the highest number ever of incidents of self-mutilation, prisoners cutting themselves, gouging out parts of themselves – 1,559 such incidents. Self-injury is not an inevitable response to imprisonment. The Social Services Select Committee visited Hinseberg, the only closed prison for women in Sweden, where some of the most disturbed women in the country are held. At Hinseberg they have had no incidences of self-mutilation. "The difference between Hinseberg and, say, Holloway," according to the Committee, "is that it is a pleasant environment with sufficient trained staff and the women have plenty to do. Acting out is not an inevitable phenomenon in a women's prison."

Why is the system the way it is? The answers are mixed. Because prisoners are there to be punished. Because prisoners have to be kept in their place. Because as a prison officer that is what is expected of me and no one has ever trained me to do it differently. Because it has been like that for a long time and closed institutions are more resistant to change than most others. Certainly observers from other countries are often surprised at the militaristic, repressive tenor of British prison culture. No simple answer presents itself as to why it is so. For many years liberal-minded civil servants at the Home Office and dedicated and humane prison governors have wished it were different and striven to change it – to little avail. Each small improvement represents a battle of many years. Then luck and the right political moment are essential components of finally achieving it.

Bad industrial relations

Certainly bad industrial relations have played their part. Relations between prison management and prison officers have been poor for many years. Prison officers are the key to the successful running of prisons. However good the senior management, however dedicated the prison governors, however adequate the resources, the way prisoners are treated will depend in the end on the attitudes, the training and the self-image of those who control the day-to-day environment, filter prisoners' access to rights and privileges, allocate cells, distribute work (when there is work), hand out the little perks, such as a bathing time when water is still hot, that are available, and turn a blind eye, or not, to minor infringements of the rules.

Currently there are 19,000 prison officers, 13 per cent more than in 1980. The number has risen rapidly, not only absolutely but also in relation to the increase in the number of prisoners. In 1947 there was one prison officer for every seven prisoners; today it is 1:2.5. No formal qualifications are required for entry. After fourteen weeks, training a raw recruit can be on a landing in a prison carrying out basic prison officer tasks. Prison officers are recruited not to a particular prison but to the prison service and can be despatched anywhere where they are needed, though in fact they can also resist moves and often do at the price of promotion.

Studies of prison officers as an occupational group are few. The one comprehensive study, carried out by the Office of Population Censuses and Surveys (OPCS) in 1983 found that 40 per cent had no educational qualifications, 30 per cent had 'O' levels and a majority had a background in the armed forces. Most are men – women make up 6 per cent of prison officers. Most are white – the proportion of black officers overall is less than one per cent. Many feel undervalued by their employers, looked down upon by society at large and very resentful of the way they are treated when compared with the group they feel most closely related to – the police. Their feelings about the Home Office, their jobs and themselves emerge from the pages of their magazine. An officer from Winchester put his feelings into verse:

"Dustbin Lid Operative"

The lot of a "Screw" is no picnic
no bed of roses – or crumpets for tea.
In fact the day of the Screw is dubious
... from first slop out to visitors three.

The police and ambulance men, bless 'em,
get full praise and justly so,
the firemen, nurses and dustmen
... well, on them too are accolades bestowed.

When the criminal is sent to the Nick tho'
conveniently dispatched out of sight
'tis the Screw who lives with the danger
... the mental strain, by day and by night.

Prisons are society's dustbins
... so it was recently said,
so spare a thought for the dustbin lid operative
... as you sleep safely, tucked up in bed.

The bitterness, the mixture of cynicism and humour are characteristic and understandable coming from a group many of whose members spend much of each day in tasks like supervising the emptying of hundreds of chamberpots into overflowing sewage systems – and never knowing when the pent-up tension will lead a prisoner to empty one over an officer's head – or explaining why a pair of smelly socks cannot be changed for another few days, or justifying the cancellation of an education class or an even earlier lock-up than usual.

Most of the major events in the history of the prison service in recent years have their origin in industrial relations. Throughout the seventies industrial action was endemic. In 1973–79 the annual average of incidents of industrial action was seven. In 1975 the London prisons took industrial action without official support. In Cardiff prison in the same year occurred the first withdrawal of labour since 1919. At the end of 1975, the National Executive Committee of the Prison Officers' Association decided local branches had the right to take action on local issues. This decision gave a green light and by May 1978 twenty-six instances of local action had taken place. In the six months up to May 1979, there were thirty-one instances of industrial action, some lasting a few days and some for several months, even though six months before the Home Secretary had set up a high-level Committee of Inquiry to look into the prison service and its problems, the first general governmental inquiry into the prison service for many decades. The report of this Committee, the May Committee, highlighted how deep were the causes of the industrial unrest in the prison service. It said:

> From early in the history of the nationalised prison service, there were signs of ... divergence of interests between managed and managers. There is nothing new in prison staff feeling that those in command of the prison service are more concerned with inmates than with them ..."

These feelings are never far below the surface. In 1980, industrial action by prison officers again affected the whole service and resulted in prisons holding no more prisoners than they were designed to take. William Whitelaw, the Home Secretary, tried to cope with the crisis caused by the industrial action by pressing the arguments for a reduction in the use of custody. Circulars were sent to courts, asking them to restrain themselves wherever possible. The population dropped to below 40,000 and it is maintained that prisons were safer, more relaxed, much easier to run. Emergency legislation was introduced to permit the use of police cells for holding prisoners and to allow the Home Secretary discretion to release prisoners early if necessary. These have now become permanent features of the legislation. The drop was greater than that ever achieved by any other means. William Whitelaw himself claimed that the public was not demonstrably less safe because fewer persons had been remanded in custody. Unfortunately when the industrial action ended in February 1981, the population shot up quite rapidly, to reach 45,000 by the end of July. William Whitelaw's brave attempts to draw on the lessons of the action to make the case for reducing the use of prison came to a cruel end at the 1981 Conservative Party Conference.

Perhaps the most dramatic of the events surrounding prison officers' industrial action occurred in April 1986. A dispute between the Prison Officers' Association and the Government led to the prison officers imposing an overtime ban. As a result of this many prisons were left without adequate cover. Prisoners took advantage of the situation: eighteen prisons erupted; forty-five prisoners escaped. Damage estimated at £4.5 million was done and 800 much-needed prison places were lost. The night of 30 April was described by the Chief Inspector of Prisons in his inquiry into the disturbances as "the worst night of violence the English prison system has ever known". One of his major conclusions was "the recurring discovery of low morale among prison staff". He goes on: "Uniformed staff at almost every establishment we visited made plain their suspicion and lack of regard for Prison Department Headquarters which they felt was out of touch with the problems facing staff and inmates."

In 1988 the Prison Department introduced changes in the way prison officers are paid and prisons staffed. A new agreement with prison staff, called Fresh Start, unified the previous two-tier structure of uniformed officers and non-uniformed direct entry graduates entering at governor level. A new pay deal was introduced. Overtime, which before the changes was averaging sixteen hours per officer per week, began to be phased out. Prison officers on the Fresh Start arrangements got a much bigger basic wage for a thirty-nine-hour week, with the option of contracting in to an additional nine hours a week. The aim was to reduce all working to thirty-nine hours over five years.

The deployment of staff was also re-organised, to divide officers into groups doing specific and defined jobs rather than deployed randomly and likely to be in a different place every week. The package also brought with it tentative moves to break through the sex discrimination that pervaded Prison Department employment practices. Very small numbers of women began working alongside male officers in men's prisons.

These improvements removed many of the bad management practices which plagued the prison service for years – the dependence on overtime, the rigidities and illogicalities of the allocation of officers to tasks. It remains to be seen how far they will improve the relationships between prison officers and management and allow prison officers to have more satisfying jobs.

For a change in the prison officer's role is essential. There must be a major programme of retraining and opening up to the involvement of other related professions. Joint training with people doing similar jobs must be a regular feature. The Prison Service College, at present used solely for prison service training, must become a major centre for the development of new ideas and new training methods, drawing expertise from across a wide field. A qualification should be developed which is recognised across professions and allows prison officers to think of a career not spent wholly in the prison service.

A failure to get to grips with industrial relations in the prison service has held reform back. So has the absence of any effective framework of law within which imprisonment is provided.

A legal framework

It still comes as a great surprise to people outside the system to discover that there are no legally-binding rules about the conditions of imprisonment. Most establishments in the public or private sector are governed by rules of some sort. Hotels, shops, offices, factories, common lodging houses, hospitals, schools, all have to keep certain rules about the conditions they provide. Prisons have no binding rules about the use of their residential accommodation. A cell measuring, say, 12 feet by 6 feet and intended for one can hold two or three or four. The numbers of people per lavatory can be one to six (Bullwood Hall), one to thirteen (Leicester), one to twenty-five (Stafford) or one to forty-four (Leeds). At no point is a legal limit reached. Food can be served in the proximity of lavatories. Yet no inspectors will come along and close the food servery. In Holland the law requires one person per cell and recent attempts to modify the law failed to get through Parliament. In Britain there is no such law. Nothing therefore stands between the system and the relentless pressure put upon it except staff and prisoner resistance – a dangerous mechanism. Prison governors have nothing to appeal to when protesting that they are being asked to do the impossible, that they do not think they should cram in another 100 prisoners and then another 100 prisoners and then keep them all locked up for longer. They can appeal to morality. They can say it is wrong to keep even prisoners in such conditions. They can appeal to expediency. They can say prisoners will catch infectious diseases; prisoners will riot. They cannot appeal to any laws or regulations because there are no effective legal remedies.

This is why staff are such strong supporters of the withdrawal of Crown immunity from prisons and for a code of minimum standards. Crown immunity means in effect that no proceedings, either criminal or civil, can be brought against the Crown. When conditions in Crown buildings fail to meet the standards required by, for example, the 1984 Food Act or the 1974 Health and Safety at Work Act, those responsible cannot be taken to court. This is the case even when the conditions could result in serious illness, injury or death. Immunity from the Food Act means that local authority environmental health officers have no right to inspect prison kitchens. The Home Office argues that this task belongs to the prison medical officers who should "maintain informal contact" with local authority environmental health officers. The prison medical officers themselves do not see this arrangement as an answer. Speaking through their organisation, the Prison Medical Association, they told the Social Services Select Committee:

> It would be logical for the Home Office either to open its doors to local health authority community physicians and environmental health inspectors or to appoint such officers of its own to ensure that the hygiene of prison establishments falls into line with other buildings which are not Crown property.

The Select Committee, having heard a range of evidence from all interested parties, including the Home Office, strongly in favour of the status quo, concluded that Crown immunity should be removed from prison kitchens and hospitals.

The Chief Inspector of Prisons, who reports regularly on the state of prison kitchens, referred in his 1985 annual report to the outbreak of salmonella poisoning at Leeds prison in 1985 and concluded: "If public confidence in the standards of hygiene applied to public institutions, such as prisons, is to be maintained, it may well be that the ending of Crown immunity is the price that will have to be paid."

At Wandsworth prison, the central washing-up area on Wing B2 was so appalling that in the view of a Board member who is an environmental health officer, "if Crown immunity did not exist, since it is considered as part of a food room, it would be closed immediately".

Health and safety is also a key question for those who work in prisons. The provisions of the Health and Safety at Work Act apply to prisons and inspectors from the Health and Safety Executive have the right to enter prisons and pay regular visits. However, Crown immunity prevents prosecution of the prison authorities if they fail to comply with the Act. The Health and Safety Commission has long pressed the view that the Crown should not be immune from enforcement and prosecution. Having failed to make any headway with this argument, the Commission has introduced a system of Crown enforcement notices which are the equivalent of the notice the inspectors could serve on an employer in the private sector. The Prison Officers' Association has expressed its concern strongly: "We cannot envisage a situation in any non-Crown property where conditions such as those in which prison staff and prisoners are obliged to live and work would be tolerated."

Their anxiety is understandable when considering but one example of what can happen. On 9 May 1987, two prison officers working to clear the blockage in the sewage pumping station at Stocken prison, a new establishment opened in 1985, were overcome by toxic fumes and had to be taken to hospital. As a result the Health and Safety Executive issued a notice prohibiting entry to the premises without breathing apparatus. The POA claims that before and after the incident, numerous breaches of the Health and Safety Act occurred.

The sewage pumping station was not the only problem at Stocken. The prison farm, formerly a part of Ashwell prison, about a mile away, where prisoners worked to produce food for the prison service, so shocked the Inspectorate that they asked the Home Office Health and Safety Officer to visit the farm and report on it. The building housing the facilities for the prisoners whilst at work was in imminent danger of collapse. The roof leaked. The drains were blocked. There was a smell of "faecal contamination". The dairy had no toilet facilities. Prisoners either had to walk a quarter of a mile or "relieve" themselves in convenient places around the farm. This provided conditions for propagating salmonella and Hepatitis A. Toxic materials were kept in a cupboard with many other materials from which they should be kept separate. No facilities were available for washing the body or eyes of anyone contaminated by a toxic material.

It appeared that the representations about the conditions on the farm had been made to senior levels in the prison service since 1979.

The medical officer had raised the question of the conditions in the prisoners' Portakabin. Nothing had been done.

At Hull, the Board of Visitors report for 1987 complained that:

> nothing has been done during the year to deal with the fire hazard in this wing (the youth wing) identified by the Fire Inspector as long ago as 1987. In March 1987, in response to representations made by the Board to the Prison Department Headquarters, a specific promise was made in writing that the necessary work would be dealt with by the end of the year. Nothing has been done ...

The Government position on Crown immunity is not shaken by such revelations. Replying to the Home Affairs Select Committee recommendation that Crown immunity should be phased out, the Home Office points out that it would really be superfluous because it already behaves as if it were subject to the law. It is, they say, "Government policy" to comply with the enforcement provisions of the Health and Safety at Work 1974 Act. It is "Government policy" in catering facilities to meet "the hygiene standards laid down in the legislation". Also, perhaps in recognition of the slightly hollow ring of these assurances, the Home Office asserts that DHSS environmental health officers and inspectors from the Health and Safety Executive sometimes inspect prisons. Furthermore, the medical officers inspect their prisons twice a year, in June and December. And finally, if there is "demonstrable need", as for example "an outbreak of an infectious disease", they can invite an inspection by the "Local Environmental Health Authority". They conclude, the Government is not "persuaded that there is anything to be gained from the removal of Crown immunity from prison establishments".

Whilst the removal of Crown immunity would have some effect on improving conditions, there is wide agreement that substantial progress cannot be made until there is a code of minimum standards for prisons. Over the past six years support for the introduction of an official code of minimum standards has been growing fast. The prison governors, through their trade union, have taken the lead in advocating that minimum standards based on the European Prison Rules should be incorporated into English Law. The Chief Inspector of Prisons drew attention in the very first inspectorate annual report to the need for standards:

> We regret that there are few specific binding standards of entitlement which have been approved by Parliament covering such matters as the size of the cell to which an inmate is entitled or the hours he must spend outside it, and which would serve as guidelines for us.

Since then the call has been repeated regularly. In March 1984

NACRO published a draft code showing how standards applicable to prisons in England and Wales could be drawn up. The NACRO code draws on existing legislation and standards for residential establishments similar to prisons and covers accommodation, hygiene, food, exercise and recreation and safety.

Support for a code of standards comes from a variety of sources. As well as the prison governors and NACRO, the Prison Officers' Association is in support, as is the TUC, the Parliamentary All-Party Penal Affairs Group, the annual conference of prison Boards of Visitors, the probation organisations, the Prison Reform Trust, the Howard League, the lawyers' organisation, Justice, and the NCCL. More surprisingly perhaps, the Home Affairs Select Committee, with a Conservative majority, came out in its 1987 report on prisons, albeit half-heartedly, for minimum standards:

> On balance, and in spite of the overcrowding, we believe that enforceable minimum standards and the abolition of Crown immunity should be given a chance to show whether they have a helpful contribution to make.

They go on to recommend application of standards to "such matters as cell occupancy rates, integral sanitation, access to work and recreation and food". Being realistic about the difficulties of implementation they suggest the way forward would be for the Prison Department to show where they could not meet the standards currently. It would then be up to the courts to lay down a time limit for meeting the standards.

The Government, of course, is deeply opposed to a code of minimum standards. It was not always so. In June 1982 in response to an amendment on minimum standards tabled in the House of Lords to the Criminal Justice Bill, Lord Elton announced that the Home Secretary had indeed commissioned a code of standards from his officials as a basis for discussion. When it had been refined in the light of discussion, the Home Secretary would intend to put it before Parliament to give it "full consideration".

By the end of the following year it began to become clear that somewhere, minds had been changed. No code was going to appear. The truth came out in December 1983 when Lord Elton had to make the announcement that there was after all to be no code, just – which could not be more irrelevant to improving conditions in the old Victorian prisons – an account of the building standards for the new prisons. What had happened between June 1982 and December 1983? There had been a General Election and William Whitelaw had been replaced as Home Secretary by Leon Brittan.

The lack of any legal framework does not only apply to a prisoner's right to certain conditions. Prisoners' rights exist in the same limbo.

The Prison Officers' Association, in a document called "Prisoners Rights – real or imagined?" (1986) talks of "the scattered, partial and unenforceable obligations owed by the prison authorities to prisoners". The courts have moved painfully slowly in admitting that they have any jurisdiction over what happens to prisoners. The spirit of Lord Denning's famous comment, made in 1972, "If the courts were to entertain actions from disgruntled prisoners, the governor's life would be made intolerable. The discipline of the prison would be undermined" lives on. However, gradually, inroads have been made. In 1978, the Court of Appeal agreed that prisoners dissatisfied with the way they had been treated at disciplinary proceedings before Boards of Visitors could ask the courts to review the case. In 1982 the House of Lords ruled that the governor of Albany prison, Colin Honey, was in contempt of court by preventing a prisoner, Stephen Raymond, from taking legal proceedings. They made the statement: "A convicted prisoner retains all civil rights which are not taken away expressly or by necessary implication."

In 1984, in the Tarrant judgement, the Divisional Court ruled that Boards of Visitors had the discretion to allow a prisoner legal representation at a disciplinary hearing and set out the guidelines they should follow in using this discretion. This caused some consternation since the Home Office had always been adamant that the Boards had no power to grant legal representation.

In 1988, the House of Lords decided that there was no distinction between disciplinary hearings before Boards of Visitors and governors. Prisoners could also go to court if a disciplinary hearing before a governor was unfair.

At this rate of progress, it will be the end of the century at least before there are any significant developments in the other vital area for prisoners, administrative decisions. Here the prison authorities have no oversight from the law. Prisoners are but packages to be moved, fitted in, transported, a piece of the prison population to be "tactically managed" (as it is called). In 1978, Lord Justice Waller made it clear that there were many important areas where the court would *not* intervene, including moving prisoners from one prison to another, categorising them A, B, C or D or segregating them under Prison Rule 43. Since then, two important cases have established the beginning of a new approach. Mr McAvoy was a remand prisoner, who complained that he should not have been moved from London to Winchester. He could not, he argued, continue to have visits from his parents because they were too ill to travel to Winchester. Furthermore, his lawyer could not prepare his case properly. He lost the case but the important principle was established that the courts could rule on whether the decision was in accordance with the Prison Rules. A similar case was brought on behalf of a young woman prisoner with a baby who was transferred to a youth custody centre and therefore had her baby taken away from her. The case was also lost but the court accepted that such decisions had to be made in a fair way according to the rules of natural justice.

The weakness of the legal framework for imprisonment and the reluctance of the courts to become more involved removes a lever for reform that has been very significant elsewhere. In the United States for instance, prisoners can bring "class actions" on constitutional grounds, about prison conditions. If the class action has merit, the courts then impose orders. They may require changes to be made within a certain time. If necessary they may appoint officials to go into the prison and oversee the implementation of the changes. The suit can be settled out of court by a consent decree stipulating changes within a set timetable. In extreme instances they may even order the closure of a prison establishment, the Tombs detention facilities in New York City being one noted example. In West Germany, following a new Prison Act passed in 1977 prisoners have the right to complain to special panels of the regional court about many aspects of their prison conditions.

Of course it could be asked, "why is it so necessary to have a framework of law in order to make anything change for the better?". Surely, the system is accountable to an elected Parliament, under the direct control of a minister, who can change anything he or she likes, who can improve buildings, abolish slopping out, give prisoners some rights.

Structural change

Indeed this is the constitutional position. Unfortunately the history of the last twenty years suggests that this simple-minded, if accurate, view of the position has not got us very far. Home Secretaries, both Labour and Conservative, have struggled and failed to bring down the use of prison, create decent prison conditions, develop a highly-trained flexible staff or eliminate the oppressive use of power over prisoners. Some, for example Roy Jenkins or Merlyn Rees between 1974 and 1979 and William Whitelaw between 1979 and 1983, have genuinely wished to do these things. Some have made improvements. Some have had improvements thrust upon them. But overall, in the past twenty years, very little progress has been made on the major problems that beset the prisons. Parliamentary control and accountability is clearly not enough to ensure that change happens. The existing structure cannot deliver. Parliament has in fact allowed the poor conditions for staff and prisoners by exempting prisons from the relevant legislation.

There must therefore be a fundamental structural change in how the system is administered to free it from the shackles of its history. The major change has two components. First, a framework of law must be created which governs imprisonment. Second, a body must be established to run the prison system at one remove from Government. Plans will have to be drawn up for an overhaul of existing prisons legislation and for a new Prisons Act. The Act will contain minimum standards for the accommodation and treatment of prisoners and specify clearly prisoners' rights and duties, the rights and duties of the prison authorities and the remedies available in law. Rules will have to be drawn up specifying minima for physical conditions, e.g. cell space, natural light, ventilation, for access to bathing and sanitary facilities and clean clothes, and for activities, e.g. time spent out of cell, exercise, recreation. A right to spend the day constructively, either in work or in education, will be specified. Access to education and medical treatment shall be a right, as will be the use of the telephone and the choice to live in a single cell. The minimum standards need to be brought in progressively according to a timetable, but implementation must take no longer than five years.

As failure to meet the standards and obligations could be the basis of court action, the courts will thus assume a powerful role. Judges will become involved in prisons, not just through sending people to them but also as the upholders of standards and defenders of prisoners' rights.

The second component of the change is a new organisational structure. To manage an organisation of 30,000 employees through a central civil service department, albeit divided into four administrative regions, through a complicated machinery of Prison Rules which are not exactly rules, Standing Orders and Circular Instructions which interpret the Rules and the Standing Orders, does not produce best results. Having to balance the imperative of protecting the Minister from embarrassment with the need to allow innovation and experiment puts officials in an impossible dilemma where caution always wins.

To trammel employees' participation in community and public life with civil service restrictions feeds the notion of the separation of the prison and encourages the public in its desire to put awkward problems behind high walls and forget about them. The Act will therefore establish a new body to run the prison system within the clear framework of law set out in the Act. The body will be appointed by the Home Secretary. It will contain in its membership certain specified categories of people, e.g. a judge, a person with experience of managing large organisations, a person with knowledge of prisoners' welfare, possibly a psychiatrist. The body would be chaired by someone with a public profile, able to speak out on behalf of the prison service and participate energetically in any public debate about imprisonment.

A new framework of law and a different organisational structure should enable a new-style prison system to emerge, less at the mercy of day-to-day political pressures and required to maintain minimum standards. A new organisation should also be able to respond more flexibly to the different groups it caters for. The women's prison system must be given a separate identity within the new structure, with its own director and Advisory Board. It must be able to concentrate expertise and commitment and draw on a wide range of outside support. A similar special department to deal with young people in prison, covering all those under twenty-one, must be set up.

Physical change

These fundamental structural changes will take some time. Whilst the groundwork to implement them is being undertaken, some immediate reforms must be made. The disgusting physical conditions must be tackled.

This is not only because of the inhumanity and degradation. It will also send a signal to the whole prison system that at last its pleas have been heard. It will show that staff are no longer expected to work in conditions that would be unlawful if the law applied. It would encourage the system to believe that change is possible. With the freeze on building new prisons, resources will be released for refurbishment. A crash programme of installing sanitation in cells must be started with a target date of two years for all prisoners to have access to lavatories. Plans are already available for how this could be done. Various systems have been tried. At Stafford prison a wing has been refurbished with every third cell being converted into a washroom to be shared by the cells on either side of it. At Blundeston an electronic unlocking system has been installed to allow cell doors to be unlocked from a central point to allow prisoners to go to the lavatory, one at a time.

To improve the physical conditions will require determination, but the difficulties to overcome will only be practical ones. It will be achievable and it will be welcomed. Once the degrading physical conditions have been remedied, however, the other degrading aspects of imprisonment will stand out even more starkly. The real change needed, once the squalor has been tackled, is a profound cultural change.

Cultural change

A change in the ethos and culture of the prison system is needed alongside the very necessary creation of a new legal and organisational framework. If either is done without the other, there are dangers. Even within a more benign and humane regime, a framework of law is needed to ensure consistency of treatment and respect for individual rights. Even with a framework of law, unless there are accompanying changes in prison staff's view of themselves and their role, prison will still be seen as a battleground where one side – the prisoners – has got a few more weapons.

A debate will need to be launched on the purposes of imprisonment. The starting point should be the European Prison Rules adopted by the Committee of Ministers of the Council of Europe on 12 February 1987. The first basic principle is that: "deprivation of liberty shall be effected in material and moral conditions which ensure respect for human dignity".

The aim of imprisonment is to treat prisoners so as to "sustain their health and self-respect", to "develop their sense of responsibility" and also "to encourage those attitudes and skills that will assist them to return to society with the best chance of leading law-abiding and self-supporting lives". The gap between these principles and current practice in Britain in most establishments is wide. Therefore, following the Council of Europe document, a statement must be produced which sets out the basic principles which govern imprisonment and the objectives the prison system should seek to attain.

The principles must cover how people, both prisoners and staff, should be treated, and what prisoners should aim to do. Following from the aims, which would be based on minimising the damage caused by imprisonment and preparing prisoners for release, will flow certain organisational imperatives. Ideally prisons must be small. The larger the institution the harder it is to treat people as individuals and minimise the damage caused by institutionalisation. Ideally prison sentences must be served near the prisoner's home, so family ties and community links can be preserved and prisoners prepared for their release. Such ideals will, however, take a considerable time to realise. Existing prisons are mainly large. Organisationally it is very difficult to keep prisoners near their homes. Such ambitions should, however, guide future decision-making about allocation and any new building there needs to be. Even existing large buildings can be broken down into units to be managed separately.

The statement that will be developed must become the basis of the training of all new staff. It must form the backdrop against which all the subsequent reforms are developed and gradually transform the ethos of the system. It must consider how prisoners are treated, the ethos, culture and basic assumptions about the relationship between custodians and those guarded. It must also consider how prisoners use their time, what they do all day and what their daily activities lead to.

Programme for prisoners

The top priority is to ensure that there are some activities; that prisoners are not idle. The inability to provide a full day's programme for the majority of prisoners is one of the most damaging features of the current system. The Chief Inspector considered that idleness for prisoners "is a dispiriting experience which deadens intellect, paralyses initiative and promotes bitterness and depression. All but the strongest willed find that unemployment accelerates descent into institutionalisation and dependency."

Inactivity not only increases the pains of imprisonment and the demoralisation of the prisoner. It removes one of the main elements that makes a prison function, an element that brings some approximation to normal life and normal routines into an abnormal life environment. If there is no work, no activity, no daily purpose, the prison becomes just a place for holding people against their will, protecting the weak against the strong and controlling the defiant. The prison sub-culture is the only focus of daily life. Therefore there must be activity. But there is no reason why that activity should be meaningless industrial work, sewing mailbags or dismantling old electrical equipment, nor should it be humiliating domestic work, such as cleaning the same piece of floor over and over again. The direction the Prison Department has taken over the years to make industrial work more purposeful has been well-meaning but misguided. Very expensive workshops have been built and equipped with machinery that few people know how to use. Because of the complexities of running them and getting prisoners to them for the required number of hours, they stand empty.

Putting industrial work at the centre of prison programmes is a mistake. Apart from its impracticability it limits the scope for treating each prisoner as an individual. Ian Dunbar, a distinguished prison governor and now a regional director of the prison service, wrote in a seminal discussion paper about the direction of the prison service: "There has to be a greater emphasis on planned activity. If activity is planned around the individual, and relies on, and promotes the relationships between individuals, it enhances the security and safety of the establishment." A recent paper by a former head of the Dutch prison service, Professor Hans Tulkens, talks not of prison-based programmes but of programme-based prisons: "A really modern programme-based prison has to be based on these three principles, namely that prisoners are seen as responsible people, that security is not necessarily the dominating end and that the individual needs of prisoners are met as much as possible."

Individual plans should be made with each prisoner and devising and operating such plans should become a central part of a prison officer's job. Doing that job properly will require the officer to go out into the community. The work, training and educational resources of the institution itself will be limited. If the institution's resources were all that was available, prisoners' programmes would be very limited. But every prison is in a community of some sort, however remote and rural, with its own adult education facilities, voluntary groups and keen individuals. Many would welcome an opportunity to provide facilities for the prison. The benefits for the prison in opening up to the local community are enormous, namely access to resources, increased understanding of prisons amongst the public, opportunities for prisoners to see and be amongst a wider circle of people than that contained in the claustrophobic prison world.

Community involvement

Opening up the prison to the outside is the principle by which services to prisoners should normally be provided. Prisoners must be entitled whilst in prison, as far as is practical, to the same standard of provision that is available in the community. Thus, there should be facilities for community groups and advice-giving agencies to come into prisons and operate a confidential service to prisoners. Citizens' Advice Bureaux and law centres, agencies giving housing and welfare benefits information and groups specialising in help with drug and alcohol abuse must all have access, facilities and funding.

Closer involvement with the world outside is also essential for the successful implementation of positive measures on race. The Prison Department's race relations policy has already established a framework. Ethnic monitoring of all important decisions, the appointment of race relations liaison officers and the setting up of race relations committees are supposed to be part of the normal management process. To deal with racism in a service such as the prison service will, however, require rather more. More resources will have to be devoted centrally to promoting the existing policies. Over time the move to an appointed Board to run the prison service should enable some black people to become involved in managing the service at the top level. Determined efforts will have to be made to increase the proportion of black prison staff from its current level of less than 1 per cent. In the meantime each individual prison will have to make efforts to involve more black people in its work by bringing in community groups and actively seeking black people to become members of the prison's various committees.

An independent medical service

In no area is the principle of opening up to the outside world more important than in relation to the provision of medical care to prisoners. The way prisoners receive their medical care has been the centre of controversy for many years. The latest study, by the House of Commons Social Services Committee, concluded: "There is a body of evidence that there is a lack of confidence in the Prison Medical Service."The Committee also noted: "The UK is the only country in the West where a body of full time prison doctors are directly employed by the prison authority."

In Scotland and Northern Ireland the position is quite different. In Scotland the prison medical service is staffed almost entirely by part-time doctors and the service is run by a medical adviser to the prison service who is responsible not to the prison authorities but to the chief medical officer in the Scottish Home and Health Department. In Northern Ireland the prison medical service is run by a principal medical officer in the Department of Health, answerable to the chief medical officer. Both systems have come in for much less criticism than the system in England and Wales.

The position of prison doctors is a difficult one. They are part of a prison management which must be concerned with the security and well-being of a whole establishment. Their duty is to each individual prisoner patient, however awkward or disruptive. Prison doctors have to certify prisoners as fit for adjudication before the punishment of being confined to a cell can be imposed. This function symbolises very clearly the potential conflict all prison doctors must face. The conflict is irresoluble. Those responsible for patient care cannot exercise such functions. Prison doctors must cease to be employed by the Home Office. The prison medical service must be brought under the NHS. To ensure that prisons do not lose out in the NHS battle of priorities, a statutory duty must be placed on regional health authorities to provide medical services. Currently, remand prisoners have the right to seek a second medical opinion. This right should be extended to sentenced prisoners.

Complaints procedures

The independent status of doctors is particularly important when they go into prisons because high walls and locked doors generate the potential for abuse and the suspicion of abuse. Where people are being kept against their will, the temptation to override basic human rights and deny natural justice is always there, not always for evil intent. Managerial convenience, shortage of staff, inadequate training and fear all play their part. The establishment of proper procedures with clear avenues of redress for dealing with prisoners is therefore essential. Prison systems that have progressed the furthest in developing programmes and staff jobs, as in Holland for instance, also have highly developed complaints procedures and access to redress for grievances. The federal prison system of Canada, which deals with all prisoners serving two years or more, has a five-level complaints procedure. There are three levels in the prison, one of which involves consideration of the complaint by a prison committee consisting of three prison staff and two prisoners. The complaint can go to a senior official in the prison authority in Ottawa and finally to the special prisons ombudsman.

A new complaints procedure must be established which is clear and confidential. The barriers to making complaints, that is the disciplinary offences of making a false and malicious allegation and repeatedly making groundless complaints, must be withdrawn from the code of offences against prison discipline. Clear information on the procedures to be followed when making a complaint must be given to all prisoners when they are received into prison. The Canadian model of an internal prisoner and staff committee to consider complaints should be considered. Clear time limits must be laid down for a response to complaints from the governor, Board of Visitors and Secretary of State. The final stage must be to a prisons ombudsman. The proposal for a prisons ombudsman had been made frequently and attracts wide support. The Chief Inspector of Prisons advocated the creation of such a position in a report on Prison Complaints published in 1988.

In other countries in which prisons ombudsmen exist, such as Canada and parts of the USA, or where prisoners' complaints form a significant part of the ombudsman's work, as in Sweden and Denmark, these officials exercise an important beneficial influence on prison administration. In Canada there has been a Correctional Investigator since 1973, with the power to respond to individual prisoners' complaints as well as to conduct investigations independently. The Correctional Investigator has unlimited right of access to Canadian prisons and makes scheduled visits announced in advance to prisoners. Notices on prison notice boards inform prisoners of the existence of the Investigator and the address to write to. Letters to the Investigator are sent on unopened by the prison authorities.

The post of prisons ombudsman must be established. The ombudsman must be able to receive complaints direct from prisoners and from other sources such as Boards of Visitors, to initiate investigations independently, and to investigate the merits of decisions, not just maladministration. The prisons ombudsman's principal function must be to investigate individual prisoners' complaints about their treatment and to make recommendations for remedying them. His or her object should be to ensure that the prisoner's rights, from whatever source they are derived – the common law, the Prison Act or the Prison Rules – are fully implemented, and also that the prison authorities' discretion over prisoners' treatment is fairly and reasonably exercised.

A new disciplinary system

The way serious offences against prison discipline are dealt with must also be reformed if prisoners' rights are to be safeguarded and justice be seen to be done. A new tribunal must be set up to hear such cases.

The argument for a separate disciplinary body is threefold. First, it is undesirable that penalties involving substantial deprivation of liberty should be imposed by a non-judicial body. Second, Boards of Visitors' responsibility for adjudications is among the factors contributing to prisoners' reluctance to approach Board members with complaints. Third, removing adjudicatory functions from Boards of Visitors would enable them to concentrate on the important task of developing their inspectorial duties and their function of investigating prisoners' grievances.

The new tribunal should consist, as the Prior Committee recommended, of a legally qualified person in the chair and two lay members. The prisoner must have a general right to call witnesses; the tribunal must have the power to compel the attendance of witnesses and the production of documents; the standard of proof must be beyond reasonable doubt; the prisoner or representative must have the right to address the tribunal finally before it considers its verdict; reports on the prisoner after a finding of guilt should be given openly as evidence; the accused should normally be seated and should be permitted to take notes. The maximum penalty available to the tribunal for one offence must be 120 days' forfeiture of remission, and the maximum for related offences 180 days. There must be a system of appeals against decisions of the tribunal.

Home leave

Such safeguards are important for all prisoners. Their introduction would create not only a more just system. They would also allow the resolution of pent-up tensions and grievances procedurally rather than violently. The system would be more relaxed, more easily controlled, and more rewarding to work in. But for most prisoners what happens in prison is not the focus of all their attention and anxiety. Their stay will not be very long. Their need to make a go of it outside will be the main anxiety. That is why links with the community and preparation for release must be the focus of prison regimes for all but the most long-term prisoners. One useful device for maintaining links is home leave, whereby prisoners are trusted to go home, or if they are homeless, to an outside hostel, for a few days. Yet our arrangements for home leave are some of the most restrictive.

In West Germany, for instance, prisoners are able to take twenty-one days' leave a year, to which they become entitled after serving the first six months of their sentence. Prisoners who are considered to be a danger to the public or likely to re-offend while on leave are not granted it. Only a small proportion, 4 per cent, of prisoners do not return on time. Swedish prisoners become eligible for leave after serving four to six months, and life sentence prisoners after two years. The first leave is for forty-eight hours excluding travelling time, with additional leave every two months of up to seventy-two hours. In Denmark, an eight-hour leave is allowed to prisoners in open prisons every three weeks and can be accumulated to last a weekend. Weekend leaves have to be requested by family or friends. In Holland, prisoners in closed prisons may be allowed six periods of leave a year of two days or sixty hours on request. In semi-open prisons, prisoners get leave every month automatically, and in open prisons there is automatic leave once a week. In addition, prisoners are allowed extra leave varying from twelve hours to two or three days for social reasons, such as applying for a job or dealing with family problems.

Home leave in British prisons must be extended to all prisoners except those in the top-security categories, and given much more frequently.

Preparation for release

More must also be done to prepare prisoners for release. Coming out of prison is not easy:

> "When you get out, you get a piece of paper, and you have to go to the social. You hand it in and they just send you away; all right, we have got your piece of paper."

> "The problem I experienced on leaving prison was finding employment and getting back into friendships, like with my parents – my father had more or less disowned me whilst I was in prison."

Finding accommodation is very difficult. Finding employment is almost impossible. For the isolated person without family, starting again and finding friends is a hard task. With none of these elements of stability a return to crime can be fatally easy.

Currently after-care is very much the poor relation in the penal system. It is a low priority for the probation service. Some voluntary organisations receive small sums of money to run hostels and other projects. There is no system and no obligations are laid on any public authorities. This must change. Every discharged prisoner must have a guarantee of being offered help with accommodation, work training or help in finding a job, access to education and some social support if it is needed to rebuild a normal life. Public authorities must accept some responsibilities for resettling prisoners. For example, local authorities should operate equal opportunities employment policies which forbid discrimination against ex-prisoners. Housing authorities should provide accommodation for people leaving prison who are eligible. Local education authorities should provide educational guidance for ex-prisoners wanting to take up education and training.

A different prison system

A very different prison system would be the end product of such changes. Security and control problems would still exist. They are intrinsic to prison systems. But they would not be the governing motive for all decisions and the basis of all priorities. A range of purposeful activities, attention to what is needed to survive after release, a real effort to allow people to maintain their links with home and family, would provide much of the control because prisoners would also have an interest in living in a peaceful institution and have much to lose by any disruption of that peace. Prisons would be less violent, less bedecked with menacing security devices and much more satisfying to work in.

Conclusion

The transformations suggested here may seem too great. Can politicians really pluck up the courage to climb over the barriers to reducing the use of prison, if at the other side sits public opinion (as it is called) with the tabloid newspapers in the lead, calling for hanging, longer sentences, the punishment literally to fit the crime, life to mean life, prisons not to be holiday camps? Toughen up, they say, exact vengeance. Also sitting there will be many interest groups, ranged against reform. Public service workers are being attacked, so they want harsher sentences. The organisation financed by the big retailers, the Association for the Prevention of Theft in Shops, thinks shoplifters should go to prison. The Police Federation thinks everyone who attacks a police officer should go to prison. Can public attitudes really change to the point where a much smaller prison population is regarded as acceptable? The answer must be yes. Public opinion surveys do not bear out the picture of a uniformly vindictive public. On the contrary, most surveys show a majority favour more community service and compensation, more parole, and a reduced use of prison for offenders against property.

Society has always seemed quite enthusiastic about inflicting suffering on its fellow citizens when they get caught breaking the rules. So in the seventeenth and eighteenth centuries hanging for offences such as burglary was regarded as necessary and acceptable. Times changed and hanging began to seem rather too harsh. Banishment to Australia for ever was a suitable alternative. Times changed again and the proponents of prison had their day. Locking up and reforming through pain was the solution that fitted and commanded wide support. The next big shift must now come, away from prison as the linchpin, the centre of the penal system, the place to be sent without question when fines are not paid, orders are not carried out, the punishment to which all others are "an alternative". Prison must become the wholly exceptional, the place it is difficult to get to, the place with symbolic value as the expression of society's deepest disapproval. Most people must receive other punishments, less damaging, with reparation as their aim, not the infliction of pain.

There must be less use of prison. But can the prison system itself change? Again the answer must be yes. The system we have now cannot be what anyone wants. No one could possibly wish to be responsible for so much squalor, depression, reduction of human beings to things to be fitted into empty slots. No one could want to preside over the emptying several times every day of many thousands of overflowing chamberpots into inadequate sewage systems. No one could want to deny even half an hour's fresh air or exercise to people locked in small rooms breathing fetid air, or decide whose job it is every morning to go round the prison yard collecting the parcels of excrement thrown from cell windows during the night, or take and lock up in cheerless and unsuitable cells women clearly suffering from mental illnesses.

Yet, the transformation proposed for the prison system may seem too great, the leap too large to make. Can the huge echoing halls of the big Victorian prisons, tenanted by a depersonalised mass of anxious-looking men, patrolled by security-conscious, uniformed officers, ever become purposeful, unthreatening places, broken up into small units with staff in civilian clothes, organising a programme of worthwhile activities with individual prisoners? Can anyone envisage in the foreseeable future the large women's prison, coping with frequent self-mutilations, controlling through recourse to the rule-book, disciplinary hearings and segregation, replaced by small units with adjacent accommodation for prisoners to spend weekends with visiting families and children? Is it possible that the closed, secretive, defensive prison establishment can become a centre for community activities, the officers in the gatehouse welcoming a constant stream of visitors, volunteers and teachers, people organising groups on, for example, alcoholism and drug abuse, representatives of black organisations, after-care agencies, sporting clubs, individuals offering to visit those prisoners who never get visited.

It is not impossible. Elements of all these changes are already present somewhere in the system. They have often been tried by an adventurous governor or staff member, only to collapse when the instigators move on. The models are there. The enthusiasts for such ideas are also there, their enthusiasm all too often crushed beneath the bureaucracy, the caution, the cynicism of the old hands who have seen it all before.

The arguments for change are overwhelming, The current system cannot be defended. Nor does anyone defend it. They apologise for it, admit its gross deficiencies but claim to be trapped, by demand, resource constraints and political pressure. So in the end it continues, and grows.

By 1996, on current non-demographic projections, there will be 68,000 people imprisoned, of whom at least one in five will be black.

More will have better access to lavatories. More may have modern cells to live and sleep in. But basically at the end of the century the system will be the same. More lives will be being wasted and more degradation and humilation will be being inflicted. Many prison staff will still be working in old Victorian prisons. Many will have reached retiring age, having seen no improvement in basic prison conditions in a whole working life in the prison service. Fifteen-year-olds will still be experiencing the harshness of the ultimate penalty the state can mete out – imprisonment. Women will be bringing up their babies in prison mother and baby units or having them taken from them four weeks after birth. And the end product will be more crime, as the experience of prison is extended to an even greater proportion of the young, to more opportunistic thieves and burglars, to a greater number of the poor – the casualties of the shrinking of the welfare state and the starving of preventive services.

No Government can wish to run such a penal system, when without enormous resources being expended, it could be changed fundamentally for the better, bring better returns in crime control, and reduce the chances of politically embarrassing disturbances, industrial troubles and riots.

No sane and reasonable society can want to go on paying for such a defective product. No civilised society can want to continue into the twenty-first century a system of inhumanity and cruelty inherited from the nineteenth.

Reform must come. All those concerned with human dignity and justice must make it their cause, argue the case for it, publicly support it and make it clear to politicians that they must find the courage to face up to what needs to be done.

INDEX

FABIAN SERIES — already published

GOODBYE COUNCIL HOUSING

by David Clapham

The public housing sector, under attack from the Government and plagued by its own shortcomings, is in a crisis which could lead to its demise. But – since 1919 – council housing has been seen as a key instrument for achieving social objectives in housing, and this crisis therefore raises crucial questions. Is council housing an effective way of achieving these objectives? What strategy should the Government's opponents pursue?

This provocative contribution to the debate over the future of council housing will stimulate discussion about social objectives in housing, and about alternatives to council housing which aim to give tenants more control over their housing situation.

David Clapham is Assistant Director of the Centre for Housing Research at the University of Glasgow. He has written extensively on council housing and housing co-operatives.

ISBN 004 4452969

FABIAN SERIES — forthcoming

COMPETITIVE SOCIALISM

Austin Mitchell

One of Labour's central problems is how to develop an economic policy which is both socialist and in tune with the new expectations of the electorate. Austin Mitchell argues that the two are entirely compatible, and that British society and socialism can be transformed by a policy of economic expansion.

Austin Mitchell is MP for Great Grimsby and an economist.

April 0 04 440431 X

FABIAN SERIES — forthcoming

CAN LABOUR WIN?

Martin Harrop and Andrew Shaw

With three electoral failures behind them, is Labour a spent force? Martin Harrop analyses what went wrong for Labour in 1979, 1983 and 1987, and gives a prescription for their success at the next election.

Martin Harrop is Lecturer in Politics at the University of Newcastle-upon-Tyne
Andrew Shaw is lecturer in Politics at the University of Liverpool.

April 004 4404328

FABIAN SERIES — forthcoming

REFORMING WHITEHALL

Clive Ponting

A 19th century institution in the late 20th century: closed, unaccountable and inadequate. That is how Clive Ponting sees Whitehall, and few people are better qualified than he to make such comments. In *Reforming Whitehall* he describes what must happen if the system is to lose this widely held reputation and become the efficient and open machine we need.

Clive Ponting is a writer and former civil servant.

April 004 4404336

FABIAN SERIES — already published

OWN YOUR OWN

Social Ownership Examined by Oonagh McDonald

OWN YOUR OWN is a lively study of the topical controversy of privatization and the public ownership – which so often falsely implies that these are the only two choices.

An intitial overview deals with the actual privatization process, including the BP débâcle and the creation of private monopolies. As the author explores the history of the idea of social ownership, she gives a fascinating insight into some successful, but very different, instances of social ownership and co-operatives in a number of countries, including Sweden, Israel, Spain and the USA.

This short book will help to stimulate discussion about policies that encourage workers to become involved in the success of the organization for which they work, or whose service they use.

Oonagh McDonald, former Labour MP for Thurrock, is the Gwilym Gibbon Research Fellow at Nuffield College, Oxford, and is well known for her articles on the civil service and economic policy.

IGBN 0 04 445298 5